EASTERN EUROPEAN MONOGRAPHS, No. IX

THE UKRAINE IN THE UNITED NATIONS ORGANIZATION A STUDY IN SOVIET FOREIGN POLICY, 1944-1950

KONSTANTYN SAWCZUK

EAST EUROPEAN QUARTERLY, BOULDER
DISTRIBUTED BY COLUMBIA UNIVERSITY PRESS
NEW YORK AND LONDON

1975

Konstantyn Sawczuk is Associate Professor of History
at Saint Peter's College

Library of Congress Catalog Card Number 74-83055
ISBN 0-914710-02-8

Printed in the United States of America

To Marta

ACKNOWLEDGMENTS

It is my pleasant duty to thank several persons, who, in various ways, have aided me in writing and completing this work. Thanks are due to the late Henry L. Roberts of Columbia University (later of Dartmouth College), under whose auspices at Columbia this study was begun; to Loren R. Graham, the late Philip E. Mosely (perhaps the kindest of all scholars), and John N. Hazard, all of Columbia University; to Thaddeus V. Tuleja, St. Peter's College; to the Very Reverend Victor R. Yanitelli, S.J. (President of St. Peter's); and to the members of the St. Peter's College Committee on Research, especially its chairman, the Reverend Joseph E. Schuh, S.J.

I am deeply indebted to Adam B. Ulam of Harvard University for the thoughtful introduction and to Stephen Fischer-Galati of the University of Colorado, who is also editor of *East European Quarterly,* for his publishing efforts.

It is no exaggeration to say that without my wife, Marta, whose energy and patience are exceeded only by a desire to help, this book would not have been completed; it is dedicated to her.

In an abbreviated form, Chapter VIII, under the title "The Ukraine: A Sovereign and Independent State? A Juridical Approach" was published in October 1971 in *European Studies Review.*

Konstantyn Sawczuk

St. Peter's College

CONTENTS

PREFACE

The primary purposes of this study are to show how Ukraine became a founding member of the United Nations organization, what significant political activities it performed there in the late 1940s, and what juristic status is to be attached to this Soviet republic in the international community. Accordingly, the work has been divided into three parts:

Part I treats the story of Ukraine's (and Belorussia's) odyssey to San Francisco, where a new league of nations was created, this time with the active participation of Washington and Moscow. The role of Stalin and Molotov in the daring and successful venture to seat at least two of the Soviet Union republics in the UN is emphasized, but the familiar figures of the Western part of the wartime alliance — Roosevelt, Churchill, Stettinius, and Eden — also appear in this diplomatic game. Part II deals with several cases which confronted the United Nations in the midst of the Cold War and in which the Ukrainian delegation displayed a dynamic interest. Only the major diplomatic involvement of the Ukrainian SSR constitutes the focus of our inquiry. In Part III an attempt is made to explain the somewhat complicated, if not puzzling, juridical nature of the Ukrainian Republic, a member of the Soviet "federation."

The principal spokesmen for Soviet Ukraine, Dmytro Manuilsky and Vasyl' Tarasenko, proved to be capable adversaries in the UN debates, and their aggressive demeanor must have irritated Western diplomats on more than one occasion. Of the two, Manuilsky was, of course, much more widely known, and his forceful and colorful personality made an impression on both friend and foe. Ukrainian by birth and builder of the communist empire by conviction, educated at the University of St. Petersburg and at the Sorbonne, he gave his delegation at least a semblance of a separate diplomatic mission. His imprint on the delegation was undeniable, and, in fact, the period of Ukrainian participation in the United Nations between 1945 and 1950 may be rightfully called the "Manuilsky era."

INTRODUCTION

When, in 1944, the Soviet Union proposed to its allies that each of its constituent sixteen republics be given a seat in the United Nations, American and British statesmen were at first incredulous, then appalled. Even in the then generally prevailing atmosphere of wishful thinking, no one in Washington or London was willing to recognize those subdivisions of the USSR as possessing autonomous attributes, not to mention those of an independent state. To the American statesmen the structure of the future UN organization then appeared to be one of the most important factors in the attempt to build and preserve a peaceful world. The Soviet proposal thus seemed to put the whole plan in jeopardy, for, as American diplomats and President Roosevelt himself pleaded anxiously with their Soviet counterparts, such a proposal was bound to raise a storm of protest in the United States. The Senate, for one, might demand that the U.S. be given forty-eight additional seats. As Dr. Sawczuk ably discusses, the issue was finally settled by a compromise: President Roosevelt acceded at Yalta to Soviet proposals for *two* additional seats for the Soviet Union republics — Ukraine and Belorussia — and those two republics have, since the UN was founded, lived happily, or at least uneventfully, as members of the UN. The U.S. Senate was mollified, and it was not even necessary to accord the U.S. two additional seats, which, as Stalin announced at Yalta, the Soviet Union would be ready to support in return for that U.S. concession to the national feelings of the Ukrainians and Belorussians. From our perspective, the whole then feversihly discussed matter of who should or should not belong to the UN — indeed some might be tempted to add, the UN itself — has not proved to be of overwhelming importance.

Still, the diplomatic passions and games of that day remain of great historical interest, and in this swiftly moving world the fact that the Ukrainian Soviet Socialist Republic has a seat in the UN may actually assume real significance. Mr. Sawczuk discusses reasons which may have impelled Stalin to advance what, under the circumstances, was a brazen proposal. He stresses, as others have done, that this was an astute appeal to the national *amour-propre* of the Ukrainians and Belorussians — an attempt after their cruel ordeal during the war to bind them more firmly to the Great Socialist Fatherland. Personally, I believe that another and determining consideration in Stalin's mind was to have another bargaining counter in the diplomatic game then going on, which was to determine the shape of the postwar world. Stalin knew the great (to him unreasonably so) importance that the Americans placed on the structure and powers of the international organization which was being conceived. Hence his manuever: he would raise objections and conditions which the U.S. would find unacceptable, but for the dropping of which Washington would be ready to make, to him really important, concessions. Thus the relief that Roosevelt and his advisers at Yalta experienced when they heard that Stalin would settle for only two additional seats in the UN, as well as at his other concession on procedures in the Security Council, was undoubtedly instrumental in the U.S. government acquiescing in the Soviet dictator's plans concerning Poland and other East European issues.

The net effect of Ukraine's membership in the UN has been until now what a realist, or anyone acquainted with the Soviet political reality, might have expected. But history has a way of moving in a way unanticipated by even the most brilliant strategists and contrivers. What was in 1944-1945 a brilliant maneuver by Stalin may soon appear to his successors to have been a grave psychological error. National consciousness aspirations, for cultural autonomy, at least, are on the rise among the non-Russian ethnic groups in the Soviet Union, notably among the largest, the Ukrainians. That shadow of independent statehood which membership in the United Nations confers on the second most populated Slavic nation in the world may one day become of symbolic importance in the pressure for some of the substance of national freedom. Thus Mr. Sawczuk's study is a valuable reminder of how a political sorcerer's formulas and incantations can sometimes return to plague his apprentices.

Adam B. Ulam
Harvard University

PART I
THE ROAD TO SAN FRANCISCO

CHAPTER 1
DUMBARTON OAKS

On October 24, 1945, the United Nations Charter came into effect. Now there was a new league of nations, operating under an official constitution, dedicated to the peace and security of the world. Among the countries that contributed to the creation of the United Nations was the Ukrainian Soviet Socialist Republic.

The presence of Ukraine — and that of Belorussia — in the newly established international organization must have aroused some curiosity, for the UN Charter's membership section (Chapter II, Articles 3 and 4) speaks of member "states." Was Ukraine such a state? Then, as today, Ukraine constituted an integral part of the Soviet Union. And yet, according to the Soviet view, the Ukrainian Soviet Socialist Republic, although a member of the USSR, was still a state among other nation-states. Was the legal argument that important, or could it not be minimized or simply overlooked for the sake of wartime Allied harmony? How did Ukraine attain membership in the United Nations? The historical record is not yet complete, but the essential facts are known.

In Washington, D.C., at Dumbarton Oaks, a series of conversations took place from August 21 to October 7, 1944, among the representatives of the United States, the United Kingdom, the Soviet Union, and China. Their purpose was to define the future shape and aims of the world organization. The Dumbarton Oaks conference consisted of two parts: the first, from August 21 to September 28, was attended by the delegates from the United States, the United Kingdom, and the Soviet Union; the second part took place from September 29 to October 7 among the representatives of the United States, the United Kingdom, and China. (1) On August 28, while the discussion centered on the question of founding members of the proposed international organization, Andrei Gromyko, Soviet ambassador to the United States and head of his country's delegation at the conference, surprised Edward Stettinius and Sir Alexander Cadogan, head of the British delegation, by requesting initial UN membership for all sixteen Soviet republics. In reply. Sir Alexander said

> that he had no comment to make on this point at this stage, but at tlthat he felt that his Government will have to discuss with the;s witlSoviet Government the question of the international status of the)f the Soviet Republics. The American representatives said that they willll havihave to think about Ambassador Gromyko's proposal. (2)

Stettinius promptly informed President Roosevelt and Secretary of State Cordell Hull of the Soviet request. Both vigorously opposed it. Stettinius observed,

> The President stated emphatically that this was a proposal that the United States could under no condition accept, and he instructed me forthwith to explain to Ambassador Gromyko that this would complicate matters, that it would present untold difficulties, and there would be just as much logic for us to ask for the admittance of our forty-eight states as it would be to admit their sixteen republics.(3)

The reaction of the secretary of state was just as unfriendly as that of the president. In his book, *Roosevelt and the Russians: The Yalta Conference,* Stettinius wrote: "When I told Mr. Hull of the impossible request which the Soviet Union had placed before the conference, he remarked, 'Are these Russians going to break up our hope of a world organization?' "(4) And Hull commented,

> When Stettinius reported it to me, I said I was amazed that such a proposal had been made. I added that no such question had ever entered the minds of any of us in the American group who had been working on postwar planning. I concluded by saying I would oppose it with all my strength.(5)

In a private conversation on August 29, Gromyko was told by the head of the American delegation that the Soviet proposal was unacceptable and was asked to withdraw it from the conference. The ambassador was advised that if his government insisted on the admission of the sixteen republics to the United Nations, it should submit its request after the UN had been established. Gromyko agreed not to discuss it further at the conference,(6) although, he did observe later in the day that the Soviet government would probably bring up the matter again in the future.(7)

Apparently disturbed by the Soviet demand, Secretary of State Hull decided to meet Gromyko personally and voice his objections to the proposed multiple representation. The meeting took place on August 31; Hull tried to convince the ambassador that the major countries would not need more than one vote to play an important role in the future international organization.

> I said to him, in effect, that this proposal would "blow off the roof." The large nations, I commented, that would have to furnish leadership and the military force for the organization would have no difficulty in getting their views listened to, whether they had one vote or many votes. The United States, I added, did not think to have more than one vote, and we nevertheless felt that our influence would enable us at all times to assert ourselves.(8)

Still not satisfied their message had gotten through, the United States leaders considered informing Soviet Premier Stalin of their views. A telegram from President Roosevelt was sent to the Soviet leader, who received it on September 1. The telegram read in part:

> Although it was made clear by your delegation that this subject would not be raised again during this present stage of the conversations, I feel I must tell you that to raise this question at any stage before the final establishment and entry into its functions of the international organization would very definitely imperil the whole project, certainly as far as the United States is concerned and undoubtedly other important countries as well. I hope you will find it possible to reassure me on this point.(9)

President Roosevelt concluded by stating that this question could be considered by the world organization after its creation.

Stalin's telegraphed reply, which came several days later, was not very reassuring. On September 7, the Soviet premier reaffirmed and emphasized the great importance his country attached to the matter:

> After the known constitutional reforms in our country in the beginning of this year, the governments of the Union Republics are extremely alert as to what attitude the friendly States will take toward the adopted (provision?) in the Soviet constitution broadening of their rights in the sphere of international relations. You, of course, know that for instance the Ukraine, Byelorussia which are constituent parts of the Soviet Union, by the number of their population and by their political importance are surpassing

certain countries in respect to which all of us agree that they should belong to the number of initiators of the establishment of the International Organization.(10)

The Bolshevik leader's message concluded with the expressed hope that on some future occasion he would be able to explain the political significance of the Soviet proposal.

Here it would be useful to comment briefly on the constitutional changes within the USSR to which Stalin referred. In January 1944 the Central Committee of the Communist Party of the Soviet Union approved the government's proposals, prepared for consideration by the Supreme Soviet, to extend more rights to the Soviet republics in the fields of foreign affairs and defense.(11) On February 1, 1944, the USSR Constitution was amended by the Supreme Soviet by the addition of Article 18a, which read: "Each Union Republic has the right to enter into direct relations with foreign states, to conclude agreements, and exchange diplomatic and consular representatives with them." The Supreme Soviet also decreed at the same time to "transform the People's Commissariat of Foreign Affairs from an All-Union into a Union-Republican People's Commissariat."(12) Since the founding of the USSR in 1923-1924, Soviet republics had not enjoyed the right of direct relations with foreign countries. The field of foreign affairs constituted the domain of the Supreme organs of the Soviet Union.(13) It is clear that the February 1944 pronouncements by the Supreme Soviet served as a legal basis for Ambassador Gromyko's request at the Dumbarton Oaks conference.

The problem of admitting the Soviet republics to the new league of nations was again touched upon during the conversation between Roosevelt and Gromyko on September 8.(14) According to Stettinius, who participated in the discussion, no settlement of any kind was reached.(15) The Soviet diplomat mentioned the subject once more on September 27, one day before the end of the first phase of the Dumbarton Oaks conversations. Discussing the question of the future general conference of the United Nations, he listed, as one of the conditions for his government's agreement to that conference, British and American acceptance of the Soviet proposal for initial membership of the Soviet republics in the UN. The United States and British representatives made no comment.(16) On the same day Gromyko's statement was reported to President Roosevelt by Stettinius. Roosevelt seemed uneasy about the "X matter" and surprised Stettinius by saying that "he had reviewed this matter with the Brazilian Ambassador."(17)

American officials tried to keep the Soviet proposal secret. Not until October 16, after the conference with the representatives of the USSR, did the entire United States delagation learn of the Soviet request.(18) Why the secrecy? Harley Notter wrote,

> By decision at the White House knowledge of this matter was closely restricted for two reasons: in order to give opportunity for diplomatic activity at high levels to persuade the Soviet Union to withdraw this suggestion or to allow it to lapse, and because of apprehension that wider information regarding it would risk creating by pressure of outraged opinion an immediate deadlock in negotiations perhaps fatally injurious to the establishment of the organization (UN). (19)

The real cause of such moral indignation on the American side is not entirely clear, although one observer noted that "the difficulty lay in the monstrous unfairness of awarding such extra advantage to one of the Great Powers and in the immediate reaction to it of the American public."(20) As will be seen later, the realization that the Soviet Union republics could not legally be regarded as fully sovereign states and, therefore, not entitled to belong to the world body composed entirely of such states, did not seem to be of paramount concern.

The response of the British delegation to the Soviet challenge is rather hard to ascertain because of the lack of documentation. However, the British view, because of the structure of their commonwealth and empire, had to be different from the American view. It would seem that London was not much concerned; neither Churchill's nor Eden's war memoirs mention anything about this matter.(21) In fact, the British Foreign Office had recommended leaving the problem to the discretion of the United States, hoping for a compromise. In one of the official histories of World War II based on British documents, Sir Llewellyn Woodward wrote,

> The Foreign Office considered that, if the question were raised again, we should leave the United States to deal with it, and say that, since the United States would not otherwise join the organization, we felt bound to support them in the absence of positive evidence that the sixteen Republics had any real independence. We were however willing to accept a compromise which did not exclude India. The War Cabinet agreed with this recommendation.(22)

In a footnote to the above statement, Woodward further noted that the "position of India was difficult, since on paper the Soviet Republics had a greater autonomy in foreign affairs." The flexible and unperturbed nature of the British response was obvious; so was its opportunism, based on the requirements of national interest.

What were some of the reasons behind Gromyko's demands? Although no strict documentation is possible in unraveling Soviet motives, a few pertinent observations can be made:

1. In his September 7 message to Roosevelt, Stalin hinted that the Soviet Union republics since the changes in the USSR Constitution were eager to participate in international relations. Implying that the republics had become states with the attributes of external sovereignty, Stalin seemed to suggest that in the world organization of states their presence would be quite natural. Stalin then reinforced the legal argument by reference to physical reality. Here, he mentioned two republic, Ukraine and Belorussia, stressing the fact that these countries were more important than some others that would be founders of the UN. Although he named only two of the republics, Stalin left the impression that many of them, if not all, would fit the description. Thus Soviet intentions were proclaimed by a combination of legal and political arguments.

2. One obvious Soviet aim — constantly voiced by United States foreign policy makers — that the USSR simply wanted more votes should be accepted as valid. There seems to be no doubt that Moscow feared the numerical strength of states supported by and aligned with the United States and Great Britain in the future international body. In the case of Great Britain no political foresight was needed to suspect her in this matter. After all, Britain was an empire composed of dominions and other dependent countries, which, after joining the UN, would usually cast their vote with the London government. Soviet leadership also had to reckon with the preponderant United States influence among, for example, the countries of Latin America, which after joining the UN, would in all probability support Washington's policies. On the same day that Gromyko raised the question of seating all Soviet Union republics as founding members of the UN, he also resolutely stated his opposition to the admittance of eight so-called "associated nations" to the UN, six of which were Latin American.(23) To save themselves, at least partially, from the unpleasant consequences of isolation, the communists were not taking any chances; they wanted more than a single vote. That the old League of Nations had expelled the Soviet Union from its ranks on December 14, 1939, was a bitter experience not easily forgotten.(24)

3. If the Soviet Union had sixteen more votes, it would also have sixteen more delegations with all due privileges and opportunities offered by parliamentary procedures. In facing disputes in the UN, Moscow would enjoy the support of sixteen other theoretically independent but politically aligned states. This numerical advantage,

besides increasing Soviet voting power, would further increase its procedural, propagandistic, and psychological value.(25)

4. Another reason for wanting the republics in the UN was not initially obvious, and must be sought in the difficulties which the Soviet leaders had with the nationalities forming the USSR. All available evidence illustrates that, during the Second World War, a considerable proportion of the Soviet population, occupied by German troops, opposed the return of the communist regime. Nationalists from the various countries, which before the German invasion had constituted an integral part of the Soviet Union, had worked toward establishment of independent states. Although the Nazi authorities, interested in colonies and exploitation, tried to discourage and suppress the national aspirations of the conquered peoples such as the Lithuanians, Latvians, Estonians, Belorussians, Ukrainians, and Georgians, these national aspirations showed no signs of abating.(26) Should these national hopes for independence persist after the war, they would pose a serious threat to the Soviet Union as well, and thus necessarily had to be taken into account. The Soviets were also afraid of the so-called collaboration of these nationalities with the enemy, and had severely punished small national groups such as Crimean Tartars and Chechen-Ingush for their alleged support of German forces.(27) It was clear that something had to be done with rising national discontent, but repression alone could not be the final answer. Would not a timely concession help solve this acute problem? (28) Seating the representatives of various Soviet Union republics in the UN might create a beneficial situation: the national pride of the republics might receive a welcome boost, and the presence of these representatives would result in additional votes as well as in many other advantages for the Soviet government.

5. The precedent established by the admission of the republics into the world organization would be useful. It can be argued that, if these republics gained some sort of recognition in the UN, their participation in other international gatherings or conferences where the Soviet government required some help would be assured. It should be pointed out that in 1944 Moscow did not have the East European satellites, and its position vis-a-vis the Western Powers was not secure; it was difficult to foresee what course of action in the future would be pursued by such countries as Poland, Hungary, or Romania. The communists had to arm themselves with as many "allies" as possible. In demanding that all sixteen Soviet republics be admitted to the UN, the Bolshevik policy makers probably had no illusions about the final outcome of their request. Gromyko began with a maximum proposal, but it must have been clear to Stalin that neither Roosevelt not Churchill would consent.

However, it *was* likely that, by skillful maneuvers and stubborn insistence, at least some of the republics would be admitted. And, although by such an act of political expediency the republics' juridical claim to sovereignty might be jeopardized, at least a partial fulfillment of Soviet purposes would be attained.

6. Finally, the Kremlin leadership wanted to see the republics as founding members of the UN because it was very doubtful they could be admitted after the organization had been formally established.

The membership request raised by Gromyko at Dumbarton Oaks concerning the Soviet republics was brought up again by him in January 1945. On January 11 an extensive conversation took place in Washington between the Soviet diplomat and Leo Pasvolsky, a special assistant to Secretary of State Hull, who was a central figure in the planning of the establishment of the UN. The talks, which dealt with issues affecting the future United Nations organization, were conducted in Russian, in an atmosphere of extreme friendliness. At one point in the conversation Gromyko reminded Pasvolsky of the Soviet request. In a top-secret memorandum Pasvolsky later wrote:

> He asked me whether we have given any further thought to the question of the representation of the sixteen Soviet Republics. Most of them, he said, are much more important than, say, Liberia or Guatemala. They have their own constitutions and deal independently with their own foreign affairs. I asked him whether he really thought that they are independent countries as we commonly understand the term. He said that, of course, they are, even though they are also very intimately connected as members of a federation.(29)

Pasvolsky did not argue the point, he said only that this matter should be discussed at the proposed Big Three Conference. The Soviet ambassador agreed, again stressing the great importance he attached of the subject.(30)

Two days later another meeting took place between Gromyko and Pasvolsky, continuing their previous conversation. Again, the matter of the republics' representation was briefly mentioned by the ambassador. Pasvolsky reported that "on the subject of initial membership, he (Gromyko) repeated that the Soviet Government still wishes the Soviet Republics to be included while it wishes the associated nations, as well as the neutrals to be excluded." The American official replied that his government "had no new thoughts on either the Soviet Republics or the associated nations."(31)

This response could only mean that the United States was still opposed to the Soviet request made at Dumbarton Oaks more than four months previously.(32) And, as the communists were still hostile to the admission of associated nations favored by Washington, the disagreement on these points between the two Great Powers was complete.

Note: The transliteration used herein is a modified Library of Congress system that omits diacritical marks. Different tables are used for the Ukrainian and Russian transliterations. To avoid confusion, established English usage, rather than strict adherence to the transliteration tables, is used in the spelling of two Ukrainian names — Kiev and Manuilsky — rather than Kyiv and Manuil'skyi.

Footnotes

(1) On the Dumbarton Oaks conference, see U.S., Department of State, *Foreign Relations of the United States: Diplomatic Papers, 1944,* Vol. I (General) (Washington: Government Printing Office, 1966) (hereafter cited as *Foreign Relations of the United States: 1944).* This volume contains, among other papers, some of the documents dealing with the Dumbarton Oaks conversations. The documents include memoranda (progress reports on the conference) to the president and secretary of state by Edward Stettinius, under secretary of state and head of the United States delegation at Dumbarton Oaks; extracts from the personal diary of Stettinius covering the Dumbarton Oaks conference; extracts from informal minutes of meetings, etc.; Edward R. Stettinius, *Roosevelt and the Russians: The Yalta Conference* (New York: Doubleday, 1949): Cordell Hull, *The Memoirs of Cordell Hull,* 2 vols. New York: Macmillan, 1948), Vol. II; (Harley A. Notter), *Postwar Foreign Policy Preparation* (Washington: Government Printing Office, 1949); Herbert Feis, *Churchill, Roosevelt, Stalin: The War They Waged and the Peace They Sought* (Princeton: Princeton University Press, 1957). See also Soviet authors: S. B. Krylov, *Istoriia sozdaniia Organizatsii Ob'edinennykh Natsii* (Moscow: Izdatel'stvo "Mezhdunarodnye otnosheniia," 1960); V. L. Israelian, *Diplomaticheskaia istoriia Velikoi Otechestvennoi Voiny, 1941-1945* (Moscow: Institut mezhdunarodnykh otnoshenii, 1959).

The reason for holding the two meetings instead of one at Dumbarton Oaks was that, as Stettinius wrote, "the Russians would not sit with the Chinese because of possible complications which might develop with the Japanese." Stettinius, 16. In April 1941 the Soviet-Japanese Neutrality Pact was signed (for five years), and, since Tokyo was at war with China, the gathering of Soviet and Chinese representatives could have been interpreted by the Japanese leaders as a violation of the neutrality agreement.

(2) *Foreign Relations of the United States: 1944,* 743 (Minutes of meeting of August 28); 738 (Memorandum of August 28 to the president). In an annex to the minutes of the meeting of August 28, referring to Gromyko's request, Stettinius wrote that "by our manner, Sir Alexander Cadogan and I both indicated our surprise and our anticipation of great difficulty from this proposal" (*ibid.,* 751).

In a footnote to the minutes of the meeting of August 28, following the words "Ambassador Gromyko's proposal," it states that "in his diary of August 28, Mr. Stettinius identified this as the meeting 'at which our Soviet friends dropped the bombshell in the form of bringing up the famous X matter during a discussion of the initial membership of the organization,' and, he added, 'We always referred to it as the X matter and kept it out of the regular minutes which were circulated, keeping a special file of a secondary set of minutes with references to it carefully guarded in my safe' " (*ibid.*, 743).

Notter, after mentioning Gromyko's "bombshell" and the unfavorable reaction of the American and British representatives, noted (in a footnote): "This Government had previously been informed in a British *aide-memoire* of Dec. 10, 1943, that the Soviet Government had requested representation on the War Crimes Commission for the 'Ukraine, BieloLivonian (!), Moldavian, Lithuanian, Latvian, Estonian and Karelo-Finnish Republics' contending that war sufferings gave them a moral right to representation. The request had been rejected, but the implications of it, taken with the Soviet announcement of February 11, (!) 1944, of the autonomy of the constituent Soviet Republics in foreign affairs, were carefully studied in the Department (of State). The possibility that some comparable request might be made in connection with the international economic organization under consideration during this period had been taken into account in a memorandum by the Under Secretary (of State) on February 11, 1944, in which he expressed his opposition to the acceptance of any such proposal" (Notter, 318).

(3) *Foreign Relations of the United States: 1944*, 752 (Annex to minutes of meeting of August 28 by Stettinius). In his diary of August 28, the under secretary noted, "I . . . informed the President of the raising by the Russians of the X matter. The President said 'My God,' and went on to instruct me to explain to Gromyko privately and personally and immediately that we could never accept this proposal. He said to tell the Ambassador this might ruin the chance of getting an international organization approved by the United States Senate and accepted publicly in this country" (*ibid.*, 744).

(4) Stettinius, 17.

(5) Hull, II, 1679; *Foreign Relations of the United States: 1944*, 752 (Annex to minutes of meeting of August 28 by Stettinius).

(6) *Foreign Relations of the United States: 1944*, 752-753 (Annex to minutes of meeting of August 28 by Stettinius), 749 (Diary of August 29); Hull, II, 1679.

(7) *Foreign Relations of the United States: 1944*, 753 (Annex to minutes of meeting of August 28 by Stettinius); Hull, II, 1679. The head of the U.S. delegation tried to persuade Gromyko to omit from the minutes any reference to his request, but was not successful. *Foreign Relations of the United States: 1944*, 751 (Minutes of meeting of August 29).

(8) Hull, II, 1679-1680.

(9) *Foreign Relations of the United States: 1944*, 760; SSSR Ministerstvo Inostrannykh Del, *Perepiska Predsedatelia Soveta Ministrov SSSR Prezidentami SSHA i Prem'er-Ministrami Velikobritannii vo vremia Velikoi Otechestvennoi Toiny 1941-1945*, 2 vols. (Moscow: Gosudarstvennoe izdatel'stvo politicheskoi literatury, 1957), II, 157 (hereafter cited as *Perepiska).*

(10) *Foreign Relations of the United States: 1944*, 782-783. *Perepiska*, II, 157-158.

(11) Y. P. Brovka, *Mezhdunarodnaia pravosubektnost' BSSR* (Minsk: Izdatel'stvo "Nauka i Tekhnika," 1967), p. 110.

(12) USSR, Akademiia Nauk, *Istoriia sovetskoi Konstitutsii: Sbornik dokumentov, 1917-1957* (Moscow: Izdatel'stvo Akademii *Nauk,* 1957), p. 405. Simultaneously, changes were made in the Soviet Union Constitution concerning the defense establishment. One of the additions was Article 18b, which stipulates that "each Union Republic has its own Republican military formations." The People's Commissariat of Defense was transformed "from All-Union into a Union-Republican People's Commissariat" (*ibid.,* 406). Appropriate amendments were introduced into the republican constitutions, including that of the Ukrainian SSR.

(13) See Richard Pipes, *The Formation of the Soviet Union: Communism and Nationalism, 1917-1923,* rev. ed. (Cambridge: Harvard University Press, 1964), Chap. VI; Merle Fainsod, *How Russia Is Ruled* (Cambridge: Harvard University Press, 1956), p. 309.

(14) It is not certain whether Stalin's telegram of September 7 was received by the White House before President Roosevelt's talk with Gromyko. However, it is very doubtful that this message could have been known to Roosevelt, for the meeting had taken place after 9:30 a.m. The under secretary of state learned about it only on September 14 from Harry Hopkins, special assistant to the president, who told Stettinius that Stalin's "answer" had arrived at the White House before Roosevelt's departure for Quebec. The "answer" proved to be the telegram of September 7. *Foreign Relations of the United States: 1944,* 810-811 (Diary of September 14). The second Quebec conference — the meeting between Churchill and Roosevelt — took place during September 11-16.

(15) Stettinius, 20.

(16) *Foreign Relations of the United States: 1944,* 839 (Memorandum of September 27 to the president); Notter, 327-328.

(17) *Foreign Relations of the United States: 1944,* 843 (Diary of September 27). The Brazilian ambassador was Carlos Martins.

(18) Notter, 318.

(19) *Ibid.;* Hul, II, 1680. On October 4, during the second phase of the Dumbarton Oaks conversations, the Chinese delegation under Ambassador V. K. Wellington Koo was informed by Stettinius, in strict confidence, about the Soviet request. The American diplomat "felt that this subject is going to be a very delicate question. He said that in all probability it will never be possible to agree to the Soviet proposal. At some later time the Generalissimo, the Prime Minister and the President may have to take this matter with Marshall Stalin. It will have to be pointed out that the whole civilized world would be shocked by such a proposal. He said that the Soviet republics are, of course, not autonomous, but are comparable to the states of the United States or to provinces of any given country." *Foreign Relations of the United States: 1944,* 868 (Minutes of meeting of October 4).

(20) Cornelia Meigs, *The Great Design: Men and Events in the United Nations from 1945 to 1963* (Boston: Little, Brown, 1964), p. 20.

(21) See Winston S. Churchill, *The Second World War,* Vol. VI: *Triumph and Tragedy* (Boston: Houghton Mifflin, 1953); Anthony Eden, *The Memoirs of Anthony Eden,* Vol. III: *The Reckoning* (Boston: Houghton Mifflin, 1965).

(22) Llewellyn E. Woodward, *British Foreign Policy in the Second World*

War(London: Her Majesty's Stationery Office, 1962), p. 462.

(23) Hull, II, 1678-1679; Notter, 317. By "associated nations" was meant the countries that helped the Allied war effort without an actual declaration of war on the Axis Powers; these were Chile, Ecuador, Paraguay, Peru, Uraguay, Venezuela, Egypt, and Iceland.

(24) See I. F. Ivashin, *Ocherki istorii vneshnei politiki SSSR* (Moscow: Gosudarstvennoe izdatel'stvo politicheskoi literatury, 1958), p. 327.

(25) See Vernon V. Aspaturian, *The Union Republics in Soviet Diplomacy: A Study of Soviet Federalism in the Service of Soviet Foreign Policy* (Geneva: Librairie E. Droz, 1960), pp. 113-114. Prof. Aspaturian concentrated his attention on the Soviet advantages of having Ukraine and Belorussia in the UN.

(26) See Alexander Dallin, *German Rule in Russia, 1941-1945: A Study of Occupation Policies* (London: Macmillan, 1957); and Gerald Reitlinger, *The House Built on Sand: The Conflicts of German Policy in Russia, 1939-1945* (London: Weidenfeld and Nicolson, 1960); specifically, on Ukraine see John A. Armstrong, *Ukrainian Nationalism,* 2d ed. (New York: Columbia University Press, 1963).

(27) See Walter Kolarz, *Russia and Her Colonies* (New York: Praeger, 1952). See also Nikita S. Khrushchev, "The Crimes of Stalin," *Soviet Society: A Book of Readings,* Alex Inkeles and Kent Geiger, eds. (Boston: Houghton Mifflin, 1961), p. 263; Robert Conquest, *The Nation Killers: The Soviet Deportation of Nationalities* (New York: Macmillan, 1970).

(28) See Vsevolod Holub, *Ukraina v Ob'ednanykh Natsiiakh* (Munich: "Suchasna Ukraina," 1953), pp. 4, 15-16, who speaks about Stalin's concession to Ukraine. The author rejected the idea that the Soviets wanted more votes; what they wanted was to pose as defenders of national rights of nationalities. The latter statement is, of course, correct.

(29) U.S., Department of State, *Foreign Relations of the United States: Diplomatic Papers; The Conferences at Malta and Yalta, 1945* (Washington: Government Printing Office, 1955), p. 72 (hereafter cited as Yalta Papers).

(30) *Ibid.*, 73.

(31) *Ibid.*, 75.

(32) In the two memoranda of Acting Secretary of State Stettinius, both dated November 15, 1944 (one written for him and the other for President Roosevelt) the Soviet demand was opposed. This demand as indicated before, was sometimes, referred to as the matter "X" (*ibid.*, 48-49, 52).

CHAPTER 2
YALTA

Several weeks after the two Gromyko-Pasvolsky meetings, Churchill, Stalin, and Roosevelt met near Yalta, in the Crimea, from February 4 to February 11, 1945. According to U.S. Secretary of State Stettinius, who was a participant, having replaced Cordell Hull, the conference was the most important wartime meeting of the leaders of Great Britain, the Soviet Union, and the United States. Here, for the first time, "the three leaders reached fundamental agreements on post-war problems as distinct from mere statements of aims and purposes."

When the conference convened, the fortunes of war were running high for the anti-Axis coalition. Battered from the east, west, and south and constantly bombarded from the air, the once-powerful German military machine was being destroyed. Hitler's Reich, after only twelve years of existence, was rapidly disintegrating. Allied military and naval operations against Japan were also progressing well. In this hopeful atmosphere the Allied statesmen met at Yalta to discuss the problems of war and future peace.

Among other significant matters considered at Yalta was the creation of the United Nations organization. Although this matter had been thoroughly explored at Dumbarton Oaks, there were still several major points to be dealt with. The UN's establishment was strongly favored by President Roosevelt, and he was unsparing in his efforts to persuade the other Allied leaders to attach great importance to the question of its foundation. On February 6, at the third plenary meeting, Roosevelt brought up the United States' proposal with respect to voting in the Security Council.(1) At the fourth plenary meeting the next day, the Soviets agreed to the American voting proposal; immediately afterward, Molotov again raised the question of Soviet republic participation. The Soviet foreign commissar stressed the fact that "the Soviet views were based on the constitutional changes which had occurred in February of last year and he did not think that this Conference should ignore this request."(2)

Molotov's approach, however, was more moderate and diplomatic than Gromyko's. He pointed out that it was not his country's intention to present its request the way it had at Dumbarton Oaks. Rather, he was asking for admission of only three of the sixteen republics: Ukraine, White Russia, and Lithuania. Molotov reminded his audience that:

> it was superfluous to explain the size, population and importance of the Ukraine, White Russia or Lithuania or their importance in foreign affairs. He said that as these three republics had borne the greatest sacrifices in the war and were the first to be invaded by the enemy, it was only fair, therefore, that these three or at any rate two be original members.(3)

Concluding his statement, Molotov expressed the hope that the Soviet proposal would be accepted by President Roosevelt and Prime Minister Churchill.

Stettinius, who was present at the fourth plenary meeting, wrote later that when Molotov mentioned the admission of three or two of the Soviet republics as founding members, Roosevelt passed him a note saying: "This is not so good."(4) After Molotov concluded his remarks, President Roosevelt asked him whether he had in mind the membership for these republics in the UN General Assembly — apparently Roosevelt wanted to be sure that the Soviet diplomat meant membership in the General Assembly and not in the Security Council. Molotov answered in the affirmative, and in order to provide more justification for the Soviet proposal, he drew a parallel between the dominions of the British Commonwealth and the Soviet Union republics. Stressing the fact that the British dominions had gradually achieved international status, Molotov implied that a similar process was being followed by the Soviet republics. He again repeated that his government fully endorsed the U.S. President's voting proposal, but that the Soviets wanted to see three, or at least two, of the republics as members of the General Assembly.(5)

Roosevelt found himself in an awkward situation. The Soviet Union had just agreed to the United States' voting procedure in the council, which was both a victory and a great relief to him. Yet Molotov had also introduced an entirely different subject into the discussion: the admission of Ukraine, Belorussia, and Lithuania as initial members to the UN. The moment chosen to present the Soviet proposal could not have been more favorable. Since the USSR had acceded to the United States' proposal, why should Washington not do the same? Roosevelt was clearly on the defensive.

He began his reply by thanking the Soviet foreign commissar for the Soviet endorsement of the American voting proposal in the council; this was a step that he believed would be appreciated by all the countries of the world. In his opinion the next move was to plan a conference which would establish the world organization. He mentioned the end of March as a tentative date but thought it could take place even sooner. As to

Molotov's proposal in regard to the participation of Ukraine, Belorussia, and Lithuania in the General Assembly, Roosevelt, to quote Robert E. Sherwood, "embarked on a long speech in which he employed his familiar tactics for attempting to dodge an immediate issue by maneuvering the conversation into the realms of irrelevancy."(6) He pointed out that Britain, the Soviet Union, and the United States had different structures and traditions. The British empire consisted of large countries like Canada and Australia; the USSR was composed of national republics; and the United States presented a unit with one language, one foreign minister, and no colonies. There were some countries, he continued, that had large territories but small populations — for example, Brazil. And there were countries having large populations but small territorial size, such as Honduras and Haiti. Molotov's request, insisted Roosevelt, meant, in fact, that if the major countries had more than one vote it might jeopardize the principle of one nation — one vote. He suggested that serious attention be given to the conference which would create the organization and to postponing the question of admission either until the time of the conference or after establishment of the UN. As the president spoke, both Stalin and Molotov began to show some possible sign of impatience, because Roosevelt's Special Assistant, Harry Hopkins, who watched the proceedings, passed the following note to him: "Mr. President — I think that you should try to get this referred to Foreign ministers before there is trouble. Harry."(7) Availing himself of Hopkins' suggestion, Roosevelt proposed that the problem raised by Molotov should be examined by the foreign ministers; together they should work on the recommendation concerning the date and the place of the international conference and also decide which countries should be invited.

Prime Minister Churchill spoke next and also expressed gratitude to Stalin and Molotov for Soviet acceptance of the American voting proposal. He pointed out that "President Roosevelt was quite right in saying that the position of the United States differed from that of the British Empire in this matter of voting" in the assembly. Churchill forcefully defended the right of British dominions to belong to the world organization, and, in comparing them with the Soviet republics, he expressed his sympathy with the Soviet request. The British prime minister said he could understand such a view; a large country like the USSR "might well look with a questioning eye at the constitutional arrangements of the British Commonwealth, which resulted in our having more than one voice in the Assembly . . ." He "was glad therefore that the President Roosevelt had given an answer which could in no way be regarded as a refusal of M. Molotov's request.'' However, not willing to exceed his authority without consultation with Foreign Secretary Anthony Eden and perhaps with the cabinet in London, Churchill ''asked to be excused from giving a final answer that day in this matter.''(8)

On February 8, Churchill telegraphed Clement Attlee, then deputy prime minister, who had remained behind in England:

> Today has been much better. All the American proposals for the Dumbarton Oaks constitution were accepted by the Russians, who stated that it was largely due to our explanation that they had found themselves in a position to embrace the scheme wholeheartedly. They also cut down their demand for sixteen membership votes of the Assembly to two, making the plea that White Russia and the Ukraine had suffered so much and fought so well that they should be considered for inclusion among the founder members of the new World Organization. The President by no means rejected this idea, though obviously visualising difficulties from the American standpoint . . .(9)

Yet, Churchill was of the opinion that the British position differed from the American one; his telegram continued:

> For us to have four or five members, six if India is included, when Russia has only one is asking a great deal of an Assembly of this kind. In view of the other important concessions by them which are achieved or pending I should like to be able to make a friendly gesture to Russia in this matter. That they should have two besides their chief is not much to ask, and we will be in a strong position, in my judgment, because we shall not be the only multiple voter in the field.(10)

Churchill then asked for the authorization by the cabinet of his decision to favor the Soviet demand.

After this fourth plenary meeting an interesting conversation took place between Roosevelt and Stettinius. As reported by Stettinius, the conversation dealt with, among other things, the Soviet government's request to admit two or three Soviet Union republics to the General Assembly, and it shed light on one apparent reason why Stalin wanted to have Ukraine in the proposed world organization and why he insisted on having the three votes. The top U.S. State Department diplomat wrote:

> In reviewing the entire matter of additional seats for the Soviet Union, the President told me that evening (February 7) at Yalta

> that Stalin felt his position in the Ukraine was difficult and insecure. A vote for the Ukraine was essential, the Marshal had declared, for Soviet unity. No one has been able to determine the extent of the Ukrainian difficulty, but we in Washington, of course, had heard talk during the German advance that the Ukraine might leave the Soviet Union.(11)

Stettinius wrote further that Stalin had explained to Roosevelt that the three votes were also necessary in order to get the approval of the other Soviet leaders to participate in the work of the international organization. Earlier, Roosevelt had been quite hostile to the Soviet proposal to admit all sixteen republics. "He had told me," wrote Stettinius, "it would be just as logical for us to ask for forty-eight votes." Now, however, due to the more reasonable Soviet request, Roosevelt was of a different opinion. He informed his secretary of state "that from the standpoint of geography and population" he "did not believe there was anything preposterous about the Russian proposal for two extra votes for the Ukraine and White Russia." It seemed that Roosevelt was impressed by Stalin's reasoning that it would be unfair to expect that in the future UN Assembly that the little countries — for example, Albania — should have the same speaking rights as the Great Powers.(12)

The U.S. president was also aware, continued Stettinius, "that the British, although they had opposed sixteen votes, would not object to two extra votes for the Soviet Union." They were in no position to oppose the Soviet demand because of the make-up of their empire. India was not an independent country, but she still would have a seat. Roosevelt's paramount concerns were to preserve the unity of the Great Powers, to win the war with Germany, and then to create the international organization.

> There would be approximately fifty seats in the Assembly anyway, and after all, what practical difference would it make to the success or failure of the Assembly for the Soviet Union to have two additional seats to represent its vast population and territory? The actual power, said Roosevelt, would rest in the Security Council and each country in this body, large or small, would have only one vote.(13)

In retrospect, it seems clear that the case of Ukraine (and Belorussia) concerning UN membership was more or less settled. Both Western leaders, each for reasons of his own, were inclined to accept the Soviet bid. For Churchill it was no hard decision, having been reared in the imperial tradition where the dictates of the British empire always stood higher than some just or unjust juridical claims. Churchill must have sensed an implied threat to his country's position when Molotov made the comparison of Soviet Union republics and British dominions. Not a sovereign state, still Churchill wanted to see India as an equal member in the international community. Could not Moscow try to hinder the British from acquiring the seats for the dominions, and especially for India? The possibility of such a move could not be easily overlooked, while, on the other hand, it could be effectively avoided by acceding to the Soviet request for two additional votes. A gesture of this kind would still leave the United Kingdom in a superior position vis-a-vis communist multiple representation in the assembly, and, at the same time, the British, with some extra votes, would be less isolated.

Roosevelt's position was different in this matter, for unlike Churchill, he had no dominions or empire with which to concern himself. After the Kremlin scaled down its request from sixteen to only two or three additional votes in the General Assembly, his open hostility and indignation underwent a remarkable change. Satisfied that the Soviet government had accepted the American voting proposal in the Security Council, and since he could not conceive of the planned international organization without Moscow's active participation, Roosevelt reluctantly confronted the possibility of consenting to the communist request. In this matter he was helped by Stalin himself, who, on the subject of the admission of the Soviet republics, told the U.S. leader about the so-called Ukrainian difficulty. That this difficulty was real enough,(14) few would doubt, but it is not inconceivable that the Old Bolshevik exaggerated its danger to win the president's sympathy. Did Stalin also try to beguile the president when he agreed that he could bring the USSR into the UN only with the acquiescence of his Kremlin colleagues who insisted on the extra Soviet votes? Anyone familiar with the political system under Stalin could hardly give any credence to such a disingenuous assertion. Stalin was the autocratic and unchallenged master of the Kremlin, and he did not need to share his absolutism with anyone in the Soviet Politburo. Nevertheless, it is clear that the Soviet ruler used the alleged independence of his associates as an effective lever to induce Roosevelt to accept the communist request in return for future cooperation in the international body. Slowly losing ground in the face of Bolshevik political skill, Roosevelt tried to justify his change of heart by telling Stettinius that, after all, the Soviet Union's additional seats would not be of any real importance. It appears, then, that pressured by Stalin and abandoned by Churchill, Rooosevelt was finally ready to compromise.

It was agreed at the fourth plenary session that the foreign ministers would study, among other things, the Soviet proposal concerning the seats of two or three Soviet republics in the Assembly.(15) Prior to the meeting of the foreign ministers, scheduled for February 8, the U.S. secretary of state presumably was provided with a specially prepared delegation memorandum.(16) Attachment 1 contained several "arguments against the inclusion of any of the Soviet Republics among the initial members" of the international organization. It would be of some interest to look at three of them.

The first argument of Attachment 1 was that only the signatories of the United Nations Declaration(17) should be founding members of the United Nations organization. Since none of the Soviet republics was a signatory to it, Molotov's request to admit two or three of the republics as initial members would be incompatible with this principle. Second, attention was directed to President Roosevelt's suggestion, made at the fourth plenary meeting, to postpone discussion of the Soviet proposal until after establishment of the world organization: "We should allow a longer time to elapse and have available more experience as to the international relations of the Soviet Republics before we consider this question."(18) Because such a request in international life was so novel, continued the argument, it should be considered by the other members of the organization before any decision was made. Third, the republics could not become members of the UN, because "the Soviet constitution does not permit the Soviet Republics to control their own foreign policy or affairs"; also "other aspects of central control over the Republics are also inconsistent with the Republics being sovereign." A note on India, which followed this last statement said that this country was not a sovereign state, but still "is one of the United Nations." The author of Attachment 1 was of the opinion that the Soviets would probably use this inconsistency to enhance their claim for the admission of the three republics; however, he suggested that the problem could be solved by stressing the fact that India was considered "as having more of the attributes of separate nationhood than the Soviet Republics."(19)

The first two arguments might be regarded as legitimate, but not necessarily the third. It is quite true that Soviet Union republics at the time of the Yalta conference were centrally controlled. The contention, however, that "the Soviet Constitution does not permit the Soviet Republics to control their own foreign policy or affairs" should be taken with reservation. As mentioned previously, on February 1, 1944 — one year before the Crimean conference — an important change had been made in the Soviet Constitution, giving the right to the republics to conduct their own affairs. The pertinent amendment (Article 18-a), of course, does not state the right of the Union republics to control their foreign policy, but it could be interpreted in this manner. And, as a matter of fact, according to Stettinius, that was precisely how the Soviet foreign commissar did interpret it at the fourth plenary session. He wrote that Molotov's request to admit two or three of the republics to UN initial membership was buttressed by the statement that "The Soviet attitude, . . . was based on constitutional changes of February 1944, whereby, . . . the Soviet Republics had achieved control of their own foreign policy."(20)

The meeting of the foreign ministers took place on February 8, with British Foreign Secretary Eden presiding. In reference to admission of the Soviet republics to the General Assembly, U.S. Secretary of State Stettinius said that, although this question called for sympathetic consideration, he was thus far unable to see how their inclusion could be determined. He pointed out that at the Dumbarton Oaks conference a provision had been drawn to the effect that each sovereign state should be given only one vote in the world organization, and so was not sure how this provision could be amended to provide for the additional votes. In conclusion, Stettinius remarked, he would like to submit the matter again to President Roosevelt, who was greatly interested in the problem and who had expressed his sympathy toward it.

Eden said that he sympathized with the Soviet proposal and would declare so whenever the appropriate moment arrived. Molotov interrupted him by saying "the sooner the better." He then stressed the fact that, although according to the Dumbarton Oaks proposals that each government was to have only one vote, Canada and Australia, two constituent parts of the British empire, were to be represented separately in the assembly. Further, amendments had been introduced into the USSR Constitution which allowed the republics to establish relations with foreign countries. Molotov insisted that "the Soviet Union was a union of states," and that the Soviet republics were developing their relations with foreign states "according to democratic principles." Addressing himself to the specific problem of the admission of Ukraine, Belorussia, and Lithuania to the UN, Molotov thought it would be needless to dwell upon their "political, economic and military importance." He advocated speedy agreement on this subject, possibly on that day.(21)

Eden believed that this matter might be decided by the United Nations, which would meet and draft an agenda in which the Soviet proposal would be given the proper consideration. Molotov maintained that Eden's suggestion should be amended to read: "the three Foreign Secretaries had agreed that it would be advisable to grant admission to the assembly to two or three Soviet Republics."(22) Stettinius, although "favorably impressed" with Eden's proposal, would take no stand, repeating his statement that he wanted to discuss the matter with the president. However, he told his listeners, he expected there *would* be a favorable answer by the United States.(23)

That afternoon at 3:30 p.m., a meeting between Roosevelt and Stalin was scheduled to take place. Just before the meeting, Stettinius saw Roosevelt and told him that at the gathering of the foreign ministers he had not taken any definite stand regarding additional votes for the Soviet Union. He also informed Roosevelt that the British foreign secretary had spoken in favor of the Soviet request. The president then said that the United States would likewise have to accede to it. Wrote Stettinius:

> At this point the door of the President's study opened and Bohlen (special assistant to the secretary of state) brought Stalin and Pavlov (the Soviet interpreter) into the room. After the President had greeted the Marshal, I stated — before withdrawing from this conference and in order to bring my discussion with the President to a close — that the foreign ministers had had a successful meeting and had reached agreements on . . . Before I could finish the sentence, however, the President interrupted me and said to the Marshal, "The foreign ministers have met and have reached agreement on today's agenda." The Marshal asked if they had agreed to the extra votes for the Soviet Union and the President replied, "Yes."(24)

The fifth plenary session of the three heads of the Allied governments convened at 4 p.m. As the meeting was convening, Alger Hiss told Stettinius that he had just seen a copy of the foreign ministers' report prepared by the subcommittee(25) and typed by the British representative. He said he had asked Eden for a copy, who gave it to him with some reluctance. Hiss found in the report something to which he, as a member of the subcommittee, did not consent: namely, United States support for the additional Soviet votes. He immediately protested to the foreign secretary that his government did not approve the proposal, upon which the British diplomat replied, "You don't know what has taken place." Stettinius noted that "it was obvious from Eden's remark that the President had a private talk with the British after the subcommittee had adjourned and before the Plenary session had convened."(26) It must have been during this private conversation that Roosevelt had made his acceptance of the Soviet request known to the

British; therefore, they had made a change in the report reflecting the president's new view.

The plenary meeting was opened by President Roosevelt. After congratulating the foreign secretaries on the success of their work, he called on Eden to report on their conference. Eden read the recommendations that were agreed upon by the foreign ministers concerning the conference on world organization. He stated that the United Nations conference for the purpose of establishing the world organization should be called for April 25, 1945, and that it should take place in the United States. He further said that the states, which at the end of the Crimean conference would constitute the United Nations (that is, those which had at that date attached their signatures to the United Nations Declaration) would be the only ones to receive invitations. The conference itself would decide which countries should be included as founding members. ''At that stage the delegates of the U.K. and U.S.A. will support the proposal to admit to original membership two Soviet Socialist Republics.''(27)

In the course of the discussion that followed Eden's report, Stalin expressed the hope that, in the recommendation of the foreign ministers with regard to the admission of the two Soviet republics, the names of Ukraine and Belorussia should be mentioned. This was agreed to.(28) In view of the fact that neither Ukraine nor Belorussia had signed the United Nations Declaration, both Stalin and Molotov wondered whether it would not be easier for these countries to be seated in the General Assembly by signing the UN Declaration. Stalin even expressed the fear that since the two republics were not signatories of the Declaration, they might be excluded from membership. The Allies assured the Soviet leader that this would not happen and again stated that they would support the Soviet stand at the United Nations conference.

On the question of which countries should be invited to the conference, Roosevelt was of the opinion that, besides the United Nations, also the Associated Nations and Turkey should be considered. Churchill wanted to restrict the invitation to the United Nations only, but he did not object to Roosevelt's view. He noted, however, that if there were to be additional countries present at the conference, then he saw no reason why the two Soviet republics should not be included. The British statesman doubted the wisdom of inviting some small countries which had not contributed much to the war effort, while excluding Ukraine and Belorussia, whose martyrdom and suffering he had very much in mind.

Churchill's concern for the republics was supported by Stalin, but Roosevelt had a different idea. He opposed inviting Ukrainian and Belorussian representatives to the UN conference. Roosevelt told his audience that, so far they had discussed "the question of invitations to separate states, that is, new countries to be added to the list but that now it was not a question of a new country but of giving one of the Great Powers three votes instead of one in the assembly. . . ." Not willing to make a decision on this matter, the American leader suggested that it would be up to the proposed conference to deal with the issue. He again assured the Communist statesman that at the conference the Allies would support the Soviet request. Apparently still not satisfied, Stalin again asked if Ukraine and Belorussia could sign the UN Declaration and thus facilitate a solution to the problem. Roosevelt's reply was that such an action would not remove the difficulty. Stalin did not press the point, and the conversation on the two Soviet republics came to an end.(29)

Although Roosevelt had committed the U.S. government to support the admission of the Ukrainian and Belorussian republics to the international organization, some members of the American delegation remained quite unhappy about the decision. After the conclusion of the fifth plenary session, a member of the delegation, James F. Byrnes, informed Roosevelt about his misgivings of the U.S. commitment. Observed Byrnes:

> I reminded him that before we left Washington he had told a group of Senators that if Stalin proposed granting membership to Byelorussia and the Ukraine, he would insist upon membership for each of our forty-eight states. The truth is, the Soviet republics are no more independent than the states of our Union.(30)

Byrnes (who in a few months would succeed Stettinius as the secretary of state) tried to draw the president's attention to the dangers inherent in acceptance of the Soviet proposal. He recalled the past unpleasant experience with opponents of the League of Nations who had argued against United States participation in its work because the British had five votes in the assembly and the Americans only one. Byrnes was afraid that a similar situation could now occur; like the old opponents of the league, the new adversaries of the United Nations organization could compare three Soviet votes with only one vote for the United States. Byrnes advised Roosevelt to correct the situation by having the U.S. acquire as many votes as the Soviet Union demanded. Roosevelt was not sure whether at that late stage this suggestion was possible, but he promised to consider it.(31)

On February 9 Byrnes had an opportunity to speak to the British prime minister about this matter. He explained the difficulties of the American position "upon returning home if there should be an agreement to give the Russians three votes to our one."(32) Churchill seemed to be impressed by the argument and stated that "he would be glad to vote for alloting three votes to the United States."(33)

Reassured by Roosevelt's interest and Churchill's support, Byrnes then appealed to Hopkins for help. "Knowing the influence Harry Hopkins had with the President, I also talked to him about my proposal . . ."(34) With Hopkins won over, the two men again went to President Roosevelt. They advised him "to withdraw his agreement regarding the two Soviet republics unless Russia agreed the United States also should have three votes."(35) Their joint effort proved successful; on February 10 Roosevelt wrote to Stalin:

> My dear Marshal Stalin: I have been thinking, as I must, of the possible difficulties which I might encounter in the United States in connection with the number of votes which the Big Powers will enjoy in the Assembly of the World Organization. We have agreed, and I shall certainly carry out that agreement, to support at the forthcoming United Nations Conference the admission of the Ukrainian and White Russian Republics as members of the Assembly of the World Organization. I am somewhat concerned lest it be pointed out that the United States will have only one vote in the Assembly. It may be necessary for me, therefore, if I am to insure wholehearted acceptance by Congress and the people of the United States of our participation in the World Organization, to ask for additional votes in the Assembly in order to give parity to the United States.(36)

Roosevelt concluded his letter by asking the communist leader whether he would support, if the necessity arose, the American request for the extra votes.

Stalin's reply was prompt and favorable. On February 11 he wrote:

> Dear Mr. Roosevelt: I have received your letter of February 10. I entirely agree with you that, since the number of votes for the Soviet Union is increased to three in connection with the inclusion of the Soviet Ukraine and Soviet White Russia among the members of the assembly, the number of votes for the USA should also be increased to three as in the case of the Soviet Union and its two basic Republics. If it is necessary I am prepared officially to support this proposal.(37)

On the same day (February 10) President Roosevelt sent a letter to Churchill:

> Dear Winston: As I said the other day, I am somewhat concerned over the political difficulties I am apt to encounter in the United States in connection with the ratification by the Senate of the Dumbarton Oaks agreement because of the fact that the United States alone among the three great powers will have only a single vote in the Assembly.(38)

Referring to a conversation which the two leaders had on this subject, Roosevelt said it was his understanding that the prime minister did not oppose additional votes for the United States. Complimenting Churchill on his thorough knowledge of the American political scene, the president hoped that in case he decided to present the proposal at the UN conference, the British statesman would support it.

Churchill's reply was as prompt and as favorable as that of Stalin. The next day in a letter addressed to "My Dear Franklin," he assured Roosevelt of British support:

> Our position is that we maintained the long established representation of the British Empire and Commonwealth; that the Soviet Government are represented by its chief member, and the two republics of Ukraine and White Russia; and that the United States should propose the form in which their undisputed equality with every other member State should be expressed.(39)

It is obvious, then, that had President Roosevelt decided to obtain some additional votes for the United States in the UN General Assembly, he would have at least had written assurances from Stalin and Churchill that his action would be supported by them.

At the eighth and last plenary session, February 11, the Allied leaders discussed the text of the joint communique. During the discussion Molotov proposed that a statement be included recommending that the United Nations conference invite the Ukrainian and Belorussian republics as original members of the world organization. This proposal was immediately countered by Roosevelt; Churchill also voiced his disapproval. The president told the Soviets that such a statement would be very embarrassing to him, although he did not explain why. The prime minister said that three members of his cabinet had opposed the idea of a country having more than one vote. He concluded by pointing out that he would need perhaps several days to consult the dominions before Britain's final answer could be given to Molotov's suggestion. Stalin then withdrew the proposal.(40) As a result, the agreement reached by the Big Three at Yalta concerning the admission of Ukraine and Belorussia to the United Nations was not mentioned in the communique.

The explanation for Roosevelt's opposition to Molotov's suggestion regarding a statement about Ukraine and Belorussia in the Yalta communique may be found in Stettinius' work. He mentioned the three reasons which apparently stood behind Roosevelt's objection: 1. The chief executive was against premature public disclosure of this agreement because he wanted to explain, before the agreement became known, his actions to the leaders of Congress. 2. He wished to give Churchill an equal chance to explain it in the House of Commons. 3. It was thought desirable to keep the whole matter secret, since there existed disagreement on the question among the members of the United States delegation at Yalta. "Some members of the delegation hoped that the Soviet Union might even be persuaded to withdraw its request."(41) Byrnes mentioned yet another reason: the need for secrecy "in order that France and China might be informed of the agreement before it became general knowledge."(42)

Although the communique on the Crimean conference issued by the Allies was entirely silent on the Ukrainian and Belorussian issue, the protocol of proceedings of the conference was not. The section devoted to the world organization contained the following passage: "When the Conference on World Organization is held, the delegates of the United Kingdom and the United States of America will support a proposal to admit to original membership two Soviet Socialist Republics, *i.e.* the Ukraine and White Russia." (43) The Yalta protocol was not released to the press until March 24, 1947; the communique appeared on February 12, 1945(44)

What did the Kremlin leadership actually accomplish at Yalta? The original request voiced by Ambassador Gromyko at Dumbarton Oaks to include all sixteen Soviet Union republics, although not disregarded, was not even raised. Only two or three additional votes were demanded. Two were obtained, for the two Slavic nations, Ukraine and Belorussia,(45) which together with Russia proper, constituted the main European part of the Soviet Union. It should be noted, that the two seats were not "obtained" at the Crimean Conference; they were merely *promised.* Yet this proved to be a decisive step, as subsequent events would show, and there is little doubt that Stalin and Molotov interpreted the Western pledge of support as tantamount to admission. The predominance of power and influence of the United States and Great Britain almost guaranteed the success of this agreement among the Allies.

From the behavior of the Western policymakers it is hard to escape the conclusion that, in accepting the Soviet bid for multiple representation in the new world league, they acted from purely political motives. In all probability, the question whether Ukraine and Belorussia constituted sovereign states according to international law never entered Churchill's mind. His actions showed that he did not consider the two republics independent or sovereign entities, merely constituent parts of the Soviet Union. He supported admission of these two countries not on the basis of their juristic status, but because he understood the political needs of another imperial power to be represented by additional votes in the UN Assembly, where majority rules. Fully absorbed in the war effort, Churchill knew the value of Ukraine and Belorussia in the struggle against Nazi Germany, and he justified their right to belong to the international organization by the contributions they were making to defeat the common enemy. And, becuase of the fact that other nations, not fully independent states,(46) were to be included in the General Assembly, Churchill, in surroundings of power politics, could easily neglect the prinicple of one vote for each country and the requirements of international law.

For President Roosevelt, too, political considerations were paramount. Finally having agreed to the Soviet request, he explained to the bewildered and obviously displeased Byrnes that he had not opposed the request because he feared opposition might have endangered the creation of the UN.(47) By acceding to the Soviet request for two additional votes, Roosevelt had violated his cherished principle of one vote for each state. At the same time, by consenting to support the admission of the two Soviet Union republics, which he viewed as non-independent countries, he was discarding juridical precepts. This, however, was not entirely unique, because the United States had already accepted the British arrangement, including the admission of India. It should also be noted that Washington wanted to have the Philippine Islands in the UN, a country which became independent only in 1946.(48)

Churchill's approval of Roosevelt's proposal that the U.S. seek additional seats can be rationalized fairly easily. Churchill had no fear from such a settlement; it would even enhance the United Kingdom's position, because now, as a result of Roosevelt's decision, not only Britain and the Soviet Union, but also the United States would be multiple voters in the world organization. Only undisguised dedication to power politics could have enabled the British leader to be responsive in the face of the manifest artificiality of Roosevelt's claim for two addition U.S. votes.

Stalin's similar reaction to Roosevelt's claims still remains a mystery.

It would appear that, after gaining a victory for the Soviet Union with regard to its multiple representation, the Bolshevik leader threw it away by his quick decision to recognize the American claim for parity. Why? Was he resigned to accept the parity in earnest, thinking that having Ukraine and Belorussia in the international organization fully satisfied the current interests and objectives of his government? Or was he convinced that Washington would not go through with its demand? Some scholars are inclined to accept the latter supposition; they maintain that the dangers or risks of both a political and constitutional nature from such action for the American government were not unknown to the Kremlin ruler. Prof. Aspaturian wrote that "Stalin was certainly aware that the political risks alone, to say nothing of the constitutional barriers, would be sufficient to deter the United States from frivolous experimentation with multiple representation in foreign affairs."(49) What was good for the USSR could be harmful for the United States. "Due to the tightly organized Party, wherein reposes political power in Soviet society, the Soviet Constitution can be more easily employed as an instrument of foreign policy . . .,"(50) but this apparently would not work within the American political climate.

Ukraine and Belorussia received the promise of Allied support for UN admission because of the persistent and skillful efforts of Stalin and Molotov. Had they failed at Yalta, the road that led to the international meeting place of nations would have been barred to these two countries. When the conference ended on February 11, no spectacular gains had been registered by the Soviets in the field of multiple representation. The achievement was rather modest, and it became even more so when Roosevelt asked and was promised his own two additional votes. Perhaps Roosevelt can be accused of unnecessary caution and even clumsiness in this instance, but never appeasement or surrender.

Footnotes

(1) *Yalta Papers,* 661; Stettinius, 139. The voting in the Security Council had first become a major issue at the Dumbarton Oaks conference and remained unresolved at that time. As finally presented by the U.S. delegation at Yalta, the voting formula specified that: (1) there would be one vote for each member in the Security Council, (2) in procedural matters seven affirmative votes (out of eleven) were necessary, and, (3) in substantive matters seven affirmative votes, including the concurring votes of the permanent members, were required, with the exception that a party to a dispute could not vote.

(2) *Yalta Papers,* 711-712. There are Soviet protocols of the Yalta Conference which contain passages dealing with these facts. However, they are very brief and do not shed any additional light on the matter; hence no reference is

made to them. See *Teheran, Ialta i Potsdam: Sbornik dokumentov* (Moscow: Izdatel'stvo "Mezhdunarodnye otnoshenia, 1967); also in English: Beitzell, Robert, ed., *Teheran, Yalta, Potsdam: The Soviet Protocols* (Hattiesburg, Miss.: Academic International, 1970).

(3) *Yalta Papers,* 712.

(4) Stettinius, 174.

(5) *Yalta Papers,* 712; Churchill, 357-358; Stettinius, 173.

(6) Robert E. Sherwood, *Roosevelt and Hopkins: An Intimate History* (New York: Harper Brothers, 1948), p. 856.

(7) *Yalta Papers,* 729.

(8) Churchill, 358-359.

(9) *Ibid.,* 359.

(10) *Ibid.,* 359-360. It seems that Churchill took it for granted that the members of the British Commonwealth would always vote with the London government. Subsequent developments in the international organization showed such a view to be erroneous.

(11) Stettinius, 187.

(12) *Ibid.*

(13) *Ibid.,* 188.

(14) See Petro Mirchuk, *Ukrains'ka Povstans'ka Armiia, 1942-1952* (Munich: Druckerei "Cicero," 1953); also Armstrong; also Tys-Krochmaliuk, Yuriy, *UPA Warfare in Ukraine: Strategical, Tactical and Organizational Problems of the Ukrainian Resistance in World War II* (New York: Society of Veterans of Ukrainian Insurgent Army of the United States and Canada and St. George the Victorious Association of Veterans of Ukrainian Insurgent Army in Europe, 1972).

(15) *Yalta Papers,* 715.

(16) The memorandum, with four attachments, was presumably written by Alger Hiss, special assistant to the secretary of state; see *ibid.,* 746.

(17) The Declaration was signed on January 1, 1942, by twenty-six states, including the Soviet Union.

(18) *Yalta Papers,* 746.

(19) *Ibid.,* 747.

(20) Stettinius, 173.

(21) *Yalta Papers,* 736.

(22) *Yalta Papers,* 737. Stettinius said that, "although the President the night before had stated that he thought the Soviet request was 'all right,' I desired to reserve the United States position at the foreign ministers meeting until I had an opportunity to check again with the President in order to be certain that he reached a definite conclusion on this matter."

(23) Stettinius, 193.

(24) Stettinius, 196. The exact time of the meeting is found in *Yalta Papers,* 766.

(25) On Eden's suggestion, the subcommittee had been appointed at the foreign secretaries' conference to deal with various topics pertaining to the world organization. It was composed of Gromyko, Hiss, and Jebb, representing the USSR, the United States, and the United Kingdom, respectively. See *Yalta Papers,* 738.

(26) Stettinius, 196-197.

(27) *Yalta Papers,* 771-772. Stettinius pointed out in a footnote that "it was

in a subcommittee that the British and Russian representatives had agreed to two rather than three extra votes for the Soviet Union.''

(28) *Yalta Papers,* 775.

(29) *Ibid.,* 775-776; Stettinius, 202-203. It seems that the Soviets did not object to the Associated Nations being invited to the United Nations conference, although previously Ambassador Gromyko had expressed opposition to the idea.

(30) Byrnes, *Speaking Frankly,* 40.

(31) *Ibid.*

(32) James F. Byrnes, *All in One Lifetime* (New York: Harper Brothers, 1958), p. 261.

(33) *Ibid.*

(34) *Ibid.,* 262.

(35) Byrnes, *Speaking Frankly,* 41.

(36) *Yalta Papers,* 766.

(37) *Ibid.,* 967-968.

(38) *Ibid.*

(39) *Ibid.,* 967.

(40) *Ibid.,* 927.

(41) Stettinius, 281.

(42) Byrnes, *All in One Lifetime,* 263.

(43) *Yalta Papers,* 976.

(44) *Ibid.,* 975-968.

(45) Lithuania's case was dropped. No explanation was given for this move, but the United States could not have agreed to seat the Lithuanian SSR in the proposed world league, for it had never recognized the incorporation of Lithuania, as well as of the other two Baltic countries, into the USSR.

(46) For example, Egypt or Iraq; see Aspaturian, 108-109.

(47) Byrnes, *All in One Lifetime,* 261.

(48) ''At the San Francisco meeting . . . Molotov angrily shook his finger at the Filipino delegation and asked 'Why are they here? Their country is not even independent.' Technically this was true. Philippine independence was not consummated until the following year'': see Robert Aura Smith, ***Philippine** Freedom, 1946-1958* (New York: Columbia University Press, 1958), p. 196.

(49) Aspaturian, 23.

(50) *Ibid.*

CHAPTER 3
SAN FRANCISCO

As indicated earlier, no mention was made in the Yalta communique about the Allied agreement to support the admission of the Ukrainian and Belorussian republics to the UN. On March 1, about two weeks after the Crimean conference, President Roosevelt delivered an address before a joint session of Congress, reporting on the Yalta meeting. His speech, like the communique, contained nothing on the subject of the Ukrainian and Belorussian understanding;(1) complete secrecy seemed to prevail. Then, on March 23, Roosevelt told the American delegates to the San Francisco conference(2) that at Yalta he had consented to Stalin's demand for the three Soviet votes, and in return for this the United States would also have three votes. He pointed out that, although the delegates were at liberty to either support or reject the Soviet request at the upcoming conference, he had informed Stalin "that if he . . . were a Delegate he would vote for it." Republican Senator Arthur H. Vandenberg, one of the members of the delegation present at the meeting, was quite displeased with the president's revelation. He noted in his diary that "we began to get some of the inside 'bad news' from Yalta today. It is typical of the baffling secrecy which leaves one eternally uncertain of what 'deals' have been made." Specifically referring to the agreement to support the Soviet bid for extra votes, Vanderberg said — a bit emotionally perhaps — that *"this will raise hell."*(3) (Italics in the original.)

Roosevelt's disclosure of "the extra votes issue" to his San Francisco delegation was done in strict confidence. Yet the facts soon became known to the *New York Herald Tribune,* which then printed the president's revelation in its March 29 issue. "The White House and the State Department were immediately besieged by newspapermen demanding confirmation or denial of this story, and the White House was compelled to issue a statement that it was true."(4) The White House press release of March 29 informed the American public that:

> Soviet representatives at the Yalta conference indicated their desire to raise at the San Francisco conference of the United Nations the question of representation for the Ukrainian Soviet Republic and the White Russian Soviet Republic in the Assembly

of the proposed United Nations Organization.(5)

The release also made it clear that the United States and Great Britain would support this request, but "if the United Nations Organization agreed to let the Soviet Republics have three votes, the United States would (also) ask for three votes . . .," having obtained British and Soviet consent for such a demand. Finally, the White House assured the public that "the ultimate decision" on this question would be up to the San Francisco conference.(6)

While the United States government had its difficulties in explaining the Yalta agreement on additional votes, Moscow's actions in this matter did not help to alleviate the situation. Even before Roosevelt's disclosure of the Crimean understanding, Ambassador Gromyko already had succeeded in irritating American officials with an announcement that the representatives of Ukraine and Belorussia would attend the San Francisco conference. Surprised and evidently disturbed, the State Department tried to hit back. It produced a message, dated March 19, to be sent by President Roosevelt to Stalin:

> Last Saturday Ambassador Gromyko informed the State Department that a party of thirty representatives of the Ukraine and White Russian Soviet Republics would arrive at San Francisco to attend the Conference. I feel certain that there must be some misunderstanding about this communication. During the Crimean Conference it was very clearly settled that these two republics would not be invited to send representatives to San Francisco and would not be separately represented there.

After recalling the agreement to support the admission of the two Soviet Union republics as founding members of the UN, and reassuring Stalin of efforts to secure his request, the message mentioned certain difficulties in this respect.

> Quite frankly the difficulties, both in relation to the effect on American public support for the proposed organization and to the attitude of other governments, seem to be far greater than I had realized. I expect to communicate further with you on that aspect of the matter later but in the meantime I should appreciate it if you would take steps to clear up the misunderstanding which had led to Ambassador Gromyko's communication of Saturday.(7)

Roosevelt's note was never sent to Stalin, however, because some top State Department officials advised against such a move. They felt that Secretary of State Stettinius should discuss this matter with Ambassador Gromyko, pointing out how "most embarrassing and contrary to the

Crimean agreements'' would be the appearance in San Francisco of the delegates from these two countries. Stettinius was further advised by his aides to instruct Gromyko to ''take this up with his Government immediately and have any misunderstanding eliminated.''(8) It is not clear whether the secretary of state had a conversation with the Soviet ambassador, but it is known that on March 29 he sent a note in which he reminded Gromyko that at the Yalta conference ''no obligation whatsoever was assumed in regard to the question of the presence of representatives of these republics at San Francisco.''(9)

The American public, of course, knew nothing about these diplomatic maneuvers. However, it was not indifferent to ''the additional votes'' problem itself, and, not satisfied with the brief White House announcement, was demanding more information. The public wondered why the matter had been kept hidden and whether there might be still other Yalta secrets. In response to this, and more particularly to the questions submitted by correspondents on March 30, the State Department, on April 3, released a considerably lengthier statement by Secretary of State Stettinius. In it, Stettinius, besides dealing with some of the other matters covered at the Crimean conference, discussed the issue of Ukrainian and Belorussian representation in the proposed United Nations organization. Making no attempt to explain why this issue had not been made public earlier, the secretary of state cited what seemed to be the reason behind United States acceptance of the Soviet request. He said:

> In view of the importance which the Soviet Government attached to this proposal, the American representatives at Yalta, having the utmost respect for the heroic part played by the people of these Republics in their unyielding resistance to the common enemy and the fortitude with which they have borne great suffering in the prosecution of the war, agreed that the Government of the United States would support such a Soviet proposal at San Francisco if made.(10)

Stettinius added, however, that no arrangement was concluded regarding the actual participation of these two countries at the UN conference in San Francisco. Finally, he announced that the United States, following President Roosevelt's decision, would not ask for the addition votes.(11)

On April 5, at his last press conference,(12) Roosevelt discussed the question of additional votes. Apparently he wanted to correct some of the reports about the matter which he considered false. Addressing the reporters, he said that ''some of the boys cannot get their facts straight. It would really be fun if I went on the air and simply read the things which have appeared in the paper.'' Then the president told his listeners how Stalin felt about the votes for Ukraine and Belorussia at Yalta.

> Stalin said to me — and this is the essence of it — ''You know there are two parts of Russia that have been completely devastated. Every building is gone, every farm house, and there are millions of people living in these territories — and it is very important from the point of view of humanity — and we thought, as a gesture, they ought to be given something as a result of this coming victory. They have very little civilization. One is the Ukraine, and the other is White Russia. We all felt — not any of us coming from there in the government — we think it would be fitting to give them a vote in the Assembly. In these two sections millions have been killed, and we think it would be very heartening — would help to build them up — if we could get them a vote in the Assembly.''(13)

Roosevelt told his audience that, when the Soviet leader asked him whether he would support this proposal, he had answered, ''yes, largely on sentimental grounds.'' Roosevelt also told the reporters that he had informed Stalin, during the course of the conversation, that, if the Soviet Union received the three votes, the United States would request the same. Now, however, Roosevelt was of a different opinion; the U.S. would not ask for the three votes. ''I told Stettinius to forget it . . . It is the little fellow who needs the votes in the Assembly. This business about the number of votes in the Assembly does not make a great deal of difference.'' When asked whether these votes had any significance, Roosevelt replied in the negative.(14)

Although Senator Vandenberg thought that acceptance of the Soviet request would ''raise hell'' in the United States, it did not. Those who condemned the Yalta agreement were in the minority and their opposition had no practical effect. In fact, the public was not so much concerned with the problem of Ukrainian and Belorussian admission to the UN General Assembly as with the American claim for two additional votes. It was precisely against such a claim that public indignation manifested itesef. Stettinius wrote that when the news on this subject ''became known American public opinion condemned any 'Deal' whereby the United States would get three votes for Russia's three, but there was virtually no opposition to our granting outright the extra votes for Belorussia and the Ukraine.'' He also noted that ''the matter was scarcely mentioned in the Senate debate on ratification of the

Charter.''(15) Robert Sherwood, author of *Roosevelt and Hopkins,* remarked that ''actually, the greatest part of the resultant uproar was not concerned with the concession to Russia but with the utter, insulting absurdity of the American claim for three votes.''(16) Sherwood was convinced that, generally speaking, the Soviet claim was not regarded as of any great importance. He praised the attitude of *The New York Herald Tribune,* which said in its editorial:

> While an assembly ''packed'' by as many as sixteen Russian votes would obviously be inadmissible, a difference of two or three, one way or the other in an international assembly of sixty or seventy members could have no possible practical significance. Even as matters stand, the United States will be able to count on the sympathetic votes of the Philippines, Cuba and others quite as surely as the United Kingdom will be able to count on those of the dominions and almost as surely as the Soviets will be able to count on White Russia and the Ukraine.(17)

It appears that Rosevelt and his foreign policy advisors became the victims of their own not too well guarded secret concerning additional votes in the UN General Assembly. While the premature disclosure of this Allied agreement at Yalta was troublesome enough, casting doubt on the Crimean conference itself, the officials in the administration, including President Roosevelt, must have been greatly relieved by public reaction to the two additional votes for the USSR. Even James Byrnes, the chief advocate of the vote parity between the United States and the Soviet Union, had to concede ''that the public opposition to Russia's three votes as against our one was not so great'' as he had anticipated.(18)

Yet, several weeks after the Yalta meeting, Roosevelt was still pondering the Soviet multiple representation bid. This conclusion is borne out by the presiden'ts intended message of March 19 to Stalin, which, although not written by him, did reflect his feelings. A passage that appeared in the quoted Hiss memorandum to Secretary of State Stettinius leaves little doubt as to Roosevelt's state of mind: ''Mr. Dunn and Mr. Pasvolsky also feel strongly that we should not attempt, at least at this time, to get out of the commitment on this subject which was made in the Crimea.''(19) Did the Soviets know about the vacillations of their ally? Moscow's decision to send the representatives of Ukraine and Belorussia to San Francisco, contrary to the agreement reached at Yalta, would suggest some suspicions on their part about the intentions of the American government. By dispatching delegations from the two Soviet republics to the United Nations conference where the problem of their admission was to be settled, the communist policy makers undoubtedly hoped to achieve their objective. They likely thought it a safe enough gamble that the two delegations would not be asked, for fear of offending the Soviet Union, to leave the San Francisco meeting. Washington's unfriendly reaction to Moscow's rather devious action in securing the fulfillment of the Crimean promise is understandable enough, but it should be remembered that the American attitude toward the Soviet Union's additional votes did not inspire complete confidence. The San Francisco conference opened on April 25 as planned and lasted for two months. The conference began with a note of optimism: the war against Hitler's Germany was almost won, and in the Far East the Japanese empire was crumbling. In this atmosphere of hope for a better world to come, the representatives of many countires of the world came to create the international organization for the maintenance of a lasting peace. Many of them might have been impressed by the words of the new president of the United States, Harry S. Truman, who, speaking via radio at the conference's opening session, said, "You members of this conference are to be the architects of a better world. In your hands rests our future. By your labors at this Conference we shall know if suffering humanity is to achieve a just and lasting peace." Also, "Let us labor to achieve a peace. . . We must make certain, by your work here, that another war will be impossible."(20)

The representatives of the Ukrainian and Belorussian Soviet republics did not appear at the opening meeting of the United Nations conference, and it was not clear whether they would participate at all. Rebuffed by the U.S. secretary of state, the Soviet Union's plan to send the two delegations to San Francisco had failed — but only temporarily. On April 26, Molotov, who headed the Soviet delegation, called a press conference at which he again spoke about Ukraine and Belorussia. Among other things, he said,

> Nobody can deny that they deserve a voice at the Conference. At the Crimea Conference the great President of the U.S.A., Mr. Roosevelt, excellently understood this, Mr. Churchill also, and I am confident that the attitude of both the United States and Britain remains unchanged. It is only just to do this for the Ukraine and Belorussia, considering their services against the common enemy.(21)

Molotov must have meant not only the admission of these republics to the UN, but also their presence at the conference, for when asked by a correspondent about their actual participation at San Francisco, Molotov expressed his hope that this would take place.(22)

On the same day that Molotov held his press conference, the governments of Ukraine and Belorussia had issued statements, almost identical in content, addressed to the San Francisco conference.(23) The statement of the Ukrainian government, signed by Nikita Khrushchev, chairman of the Council of People's Commissars, and Dmytro Manuilsky, People's Commissar for Foreign Affairs, said, in part,

> The Ukrainian Soviet Socialist Republic, on the basis of its Constitution of January 30, 1937, and the constitutional revisions and amendments adopted by the Supreme Soviet of the Ukrainian Soviet Socialist Republic on March 4, 1944, recovered the right it formerly had, and voluntarily ceded to the U.S.S.R. in 1922, to establish direct relations with foreign States, to conclude Agreements with them, and to have independent representation at international conferences and bodies set up by the latter.(24)

All this, of course, was meant to assure the countries gathered in San Francisco that Ukraine possessed what is known in international law as the attributes of external sovereignty. After mentioning some other aspects of Ukrainian national life, particularly the struggle against Germany, the statement ended by expressing desire "to join a world organization of security as one of the founder States, and also to participate in the Conference of the United Nations in San Francisco."(25)

Several days previously, the American delegation was prepared to admit Ukraine and Belorussia into the United Nations organization, for it had received written instructions from President Truman to do so. In a letter to Secretary Stettinius, head of the United States delegation, Truman wrote:

> April 22, 1945
>
> My Dear Mr. Secretary:
> As you are aware, at the Crimean Conference President Roosevelt on behalf of the Government of the United States agreed that at the San Francisco Conference the United States would support a Soviet proposal to admit the Ukrainian Soviet Socialist Republic and the White Russian Soviet Socialist Republic to initial membership in the proposed International Organization.

After mentioning Roosevelt's intention to consider both Ukraine and Belorussia among the Soviet republics in a special category and after stressing the fact that it would be up to the conference itself to decide their admission, President Truman concluded his letter by stating the following:

> In the loyal execution at the Conference of the obligation assumed on this question by President Roosevelt on behalf of the United States Government I direct you to cast the vote of the United States in favor of the admission of the Ukrainian and White Russian Republics as initial members of the International Organization.(26)

In his instructions Truman said nothing about the participation of the two Soviet Union republics at the San Francisco conference. However, on April 25 Stettinius asked his delegation to vote concerning not only the seating of Ukraine and Belorussia in the UN but also about their presence at the conference. He wanted to inform President Truman how the delegates felt about this matter. "For the first time," wrote Senator Vandenberg, "the Delegation split. I voted *no.* The rest voted *yes.*"(27) (Italics in the original.) Thus, on the first day of the San Francisco gathering, even before the arrival of the formal notes from the Ukrainian and Belorussian governments, the United States representatives were ready to back their requests.

The finale of this political drama soon followed. On April 27, Molotov raised the problem of admission of the two republics before the Steering Committee of the conference. The committee, composed of the heads of all delegations, after hearing some favorable remarks from Stettinius, Eden, and Soong Tse-vung (who was both the Chinese foreign minister and prime minister), voted for the Soviet proposal. Molotov then tried to obtain the consent of the committee to invite Ukraine and Belorussia to San Francisco, but he was not successful.(28) On the same day the second plenary session heard the recommendation of the steering committee to invite the two Soviet republics as founding members of the proposed world organization. After it was read, Stettinius, who presided over this session of the conference, asked the delegates present whether any of them would like to comment; no objections were raised, so it was approved unanimously.(29) No mention at this session was made of the actual participation of Ukraine and Belorussia in the San Francisco conference. Finally, on April 30, at the fifth plenary session, the steering committee's recommendation to seat the representatives of Ukraine and Belorussia at the conference was approved.(30) On May 6, the Ukrainian and Belorussian delegations arrived at San Francisco.(31)

It was the end of an interesting and controversial journey of the two East European countries. Neither Ukraine nor Belorussia would have received this international recognition without the efforts of Moscow and the support of the United States and Great Britain. The two republics became partners of the United Nations organization after being unanimously admitted by all forty-seven countries participating in the San Francisco conference.(32)

Dmytro Zakharovych Manuilsky, head of the Ukrainian delegation, soon became quite active at the conference. One of the prominent leaders of the dissolved Comintern, with a distinguished record of past Soviet services, skillful and sometimes brilliant, the Ukrainian foreign commissar cut an impressive figure in his new post.(33) The day after his arrival, he held a press conference at which he spoke about the work of the Committee 1, Commission I (Committee I/1).(34) It appears that on May 1, even before the arrival of the Ukrainian delegation to San Francisco, Manuilsky was elected chairman of Committee I/1, which dealt with the questions of preamble, purposes, and principles of the charter of the future international organization.(35)

On May 22, at another press conference attended by some 400 reporters, Manuilsky made a number of interesting and revealing statements which should be considered in some detail. The diplomat directed the attention of his audience to a somewhat lengthy memorandum issued by the government of the Ukrainian SSR. This document, Manuilsky said, "contains extensive material on the colossal losses, in both population and material resources, sustained by the Ukrainian people in the war against the German hordes and on the enormous contribution made by our country to the cause of victory over the common enemy." Although the countries of Western Europe had suffered greatly under German rule, this could not be compared "with what was endured by the Slav peoples, the peoples of the Soviet Union, and in particular our Ukrainian people"(36) The Ukrainian foreign commissar insisted that

> because we sustained such tremendous sacrifices and made important contributions to the cause of defeating the enemy, we are especially interested in the success of the San Francisco Conference, which aims at creating the main guarantees of peace and security for the United Nations.(37)

The relations between Ukraine and Poland received considerable attention: Manuilsky pointed out that it would be to the advantage of the Ukrainian people to have a strong, democratic, and friendly Poland. He was opposed to "the Poland of Pilsudski and Beck"; he hoped that country would pursue a policy that was in the interests of the Poles and friendly toward Ukraine, as well as to the other republics and peoples of the Soviet Union. He explained his position in this way:

> If the United States of America, with full justification, seek to

> have on their borders friendly and not hostile States, why should this right be denied to our Ukrainian people? If Great Britain too, with no less justification, wishes Belgium to maintain a friendly attitude towards her, and does not desire Antwerp to form a pistol pointed at the heart of Britain, it would be extremely difficult to deny the same right to the Ukraine, which does not want Cracow to be a pistol pointed at the heart of the ancient city of Lvov, or Danzig to be pointed at the heart of the Byelorussian or Lithuanian Soviet Republics.(38)

The place of Ukraine in the structure of the USSR was also discussed. Manuilsky thought that there existed a widespread misunderstanding on this subject which must be corrected. He felt that there was an erroneous view with regard to the relations between the Soviet republics and the Soviet Union government, based on the belief that these relations resembled those between the American states and the federal government in Washington. The Soviet Union, he emphasized, was not a state which, like France, for example, is composed of one nationality and has one common language.(38) Instead, he said, the USSR was composed "of equal national Republics" with their own constitutions, their parliaments (Supreme Soviets), their own governments, and their own national sovereignties. Each of the Soviet Union republics had its commissariat for foreign affairs which could establish relations with foreign countries. Since the Soviet Union was a completely voluntary union, Ukraine, like any other republic, had the constitutional right to secede from it.

Manuilsky said that the Ukrainian people had not exercised this right because the Soviet Union had brought economic, political, and military benefits to them: "Thanks to the support of the people of the entire Soviet Union, we have in the main succeeded in reuniting lands and parts of our Ukrainian people, which had been forcibly wrested away from us, into a single national Ukrainian State."(40)

Manuilsky tried to shed additional light on the status of the Soviet republics by saying that the difficulties were rooted in the fact that foreign states were accustomed to dealing only with the Soviet government and not with individual republics. This was because in 1923, the republics had delegated to the Soviet Union government their rights to be represented in the international arena, which they had done because they were quite weak at the time. But now, as a result of great strides made by the republics in economic, cultural, and political areas and because of their immense contribution in the war against Germany, a change had taken place in their international standing. According to the new constitutional law of the Soviet Union and its republics, passed in 1944, the republics had regained the right of independent representation in foreign affairs. A first practical step in the right direction was the participation of Ukraine and Belorussia in the San Francisco conference. It was to be expected, concluded the commissar, that in the future the scope of the diplomatic relations of Ukraine and other republics would be enlarged.

Manuilsky's statement aroused a great interest among the correspondents. One wanted to know whether the Ukrainian SSR was contemplating an exchange of diplomatic and consular representatives with foreign states. In reply, the Soviet diplomat said, in part, that "the Ukrainian Soviet Government is ready at any time to exchange diplomatic and consular representatives with any country, and of course with the United States."(41) Another reporter asked why Ukraine, after centuries of Russian cultural domination, had chosen the road of independence at this time. The foreign commissar forthrightly, with no uneasiness, answered that it was the policy of the government of the Soviet Union as well as that of Soviet Ukraine "to develop the civilization and culture of all nationalities, . . ." and that such a policy constituted "the foundation of the friendship of the peoples of the U.S.S.R."(42) Whether his answer satisfied the correspondent is doubtful, but the matter was not pursued further. When another reporter tried to ascertain whether Manuilsky foresaw the possibility of all other Soviet Union republics applying for membership in the UN, his reply was, "I foresee it to a very great degree."(43)

One gets the impression from Manuilsky's press conference that a new era had dawned on the nation he claimed to represent. In Manuilsky's statements were some of the familiar elements that comprise the national interests of any state. The arguments about national security, border problems, and the economic and political advantages arising from the association with other nations were normal enough; yet, there was something missing in these statements, for it was not difficult to perceive that he did not represent a truly independent country with its own foreign policy.

A month later, on June 26, the representatives of fifty countries signed the United Nations Charter. The new — and, it was hoped, much better and stronger world league — was established. Dmytro Manuilsky signed for Ukraine. On August 23 *Radians'ka Ukraina* reported that "on August 22, 1945, the Presidium of the Supreme Council of the Ukrainian Soviet Socialist Republic had ratified the Charter of the United Nations Organization which was signed in San Francisco (USA) on June 26, 1945."(44) According to Chapter II,

Article 3 of the UN Charter,

> the original members of the United Nations shall be the states which, having participated in the United Nations Conference on International Organization at San Francisco, or having previously signed the Declaration by United Nations of January 1, 1942, sign the present Charter and ratify it in accordance with Article 110.(45)

Since Ukraine had taken part in the United Nations conference and had signed the charter and ratified it in conformity with Article 110, it became a founding member.

It had taken one year, from August 1944, when the question of admission of all Soviet Union republics, including Ukraine, was first raised, until August 1945, when the UN Charter was ratified, for the Ukrainian SSR to become a founding member of the UN. Together with its sister republic, Belorussia, Ukraine crossed many barriers before reaching its goal.

In their march toward international recognition led by Moscow's wartime leadership, some amusing aspects in this serious diplomatic game were not altogether lacking. Roosevelt's idea, for example, to admit both republics as founding members of the world organization after it had been established is a case in point. How can one become a founding member of the United Nations without taking part in its founding, especially if there is a provision in the Charter (Chapter II, Article 3) that the original members "shall be the states which, . . . participated in the United Nations Conference on International Organization, or . . . previously signed the Declaration by the United Nations of January 1, 1942. . . ."? Since the U.S. president had also opposed the suggestion of the communist leaders at Yalta to have these republics sign the Declaration, the alternative route of becoming an original member was barred.

The event which occurred during the second plenary session of the San Francisco conference spelled the admission of these countries to the group of nations intending to create the UN. Strictly speaking, Ukrainian and Belorussian SSR were not admitted to the United Nations organization at all, for like many other countires, they were among its founders.

Even after the two republics had become members of the UN, there were still some influential people in the United States who regretted what had happened. One of them was Byrnes, who became the secretary of state in July 1945. He, of course, was a steadfast and consistent opponent of additional Soviet votes. His reasoning warrants attention. The American diplomat was of the opinion that at San Francisco the

United States should have demanded three votes for itself, as agreed at Yalta. Such an action, in turn, would have led the smaller countries to oppose both the Soviet and the American requests. "This course would have been just and it would have resulted in both governments having only one vote. That would have been the best solution."(46)

Had this occurred, the course begun at Dumbarton Oaks would have been ended at San Francisco. Ukraine would have been left outside the larger community of nations and the voices of its communist representatives would have been silent in the halls of the UN. But this did not happen, and its importance is duly acknowledged by Soviet Ukrainian writers. "Membership in the UNO," according to K. Zabihailo, "became the main element for the realization by the Ukrainian SSR of Leninist foreign policy, since the Government and people of Ukraine regard the United Nations Organization as an organ called upon to secure peace and friendship among nations." (47)

Footnotes

(1) See Franklin Delano Roosevelt, *The Public Papers and Addresses of Franklin Delano Roosevelt,* Vol. XIII: *1944-1945. Victory and the Threshold of Peace,* compiled by Samuel I. Rosenman (New York: Harper Brothers, 1950), pp. 570-586. Churchill, too, was silent on this matter in his report to to the House of Commons on February 27. See Great Britain, *5 Parliamentary Debates* (Commons), 408, cols. 1267-1295.

(2) The Allies had agreed to hold the UN conference at San Francisco. It was Stettinius who had suggested the site; see Stettinius, 203-207, for some interesting observations on this topic.

(3) Arthur H. Vandenberg, Jr., ed. with the collaboration of Joe Alex Morris, *The Private Papers of Senator Vandenberg,* (Boston: Houghton Mifflin, 1952), p. 159. The senator wrote, strangely enough, that "at the meeting Roosevelt told us that at Yalta Stalin demanded six votes in the new League Assembly (to match the 'six' of the totalled British Commonwealth, etc.)" (*ibid).* No such demand can be found in the *Yalta Papers* or in the works of Stettinius, Byrnes, or Churchill.

(4) Sherwood, 876.

(5) U.S., *Department of State Bulletin,* XII (301): 530 (April 1, 1945).

(6) *Ibid.*

(7) *Yalta Papers,* 990-991.

(8) *Ibid.* The "top State Department officials" were James Dunn, assistant secretary of state, and Leo Pasvolsky. The whole memorandum, addressed to Secretary of State Stettinius, was presumably written by Alger Hiss, then director of the Office of Special Political Affairs. It contained the introductory remarks and three attachments, the first being Roosevelt's draft message to Stalin.

(9) *Ibid.*, 990, footnote 2.
(10) *Department of State Bulletin,* XII (301): 600 (April 8, 1945).
(11) *Ibid.*, 601.
(12) President Roosevelt died on April 12, 1945, two months after the Crimean conference.
(13) *Roosevelt,* 610.
(14) *Roosevelt,* 611. The president's revelation of his conversation with Stalin is a remarkable piece of information in several respects, but in one respect, at least, it is even more curious than remarkable. A thorough reading of the *Yalta Papers,* Stettinius, Byrnes, etc., failed to uncover that part of the conversation between Roosevelt and Stalin in which the former spoke about the three votes for the United States. As far as is known, only letters on this subject were exchanged between the two leaders.
(15) Stettinius, 282.
(16) Sherwood, 877.
(17) *Ibid.* See also Charles E. Bohlen, *Witness to History, 1929-1969* (New York: W. W. Norton, 1973). Bohlen wrote that "when the idea of three American votes leaked in Washington, it was greeted with ridicule by the public. The request was dropped by the American government. I have never heard that there was any other motive on Roosevelt's part except to offset the three Soviet votes. I believe Roosevelt, ill and exhausted with days of arguing, simply made a mistake." (Bohlen, 195).
(18) Byrnes, *Speaking Frankly,* 41-42.
(19) *Yalta Papers,* 990.
(20) *Documents of the United Nations Conference on International Organization, San Francisco, 1945* (London, New York, 1945), Vol. 1, General (Doc. 8, English), p. 112 (hereafter cited as *Documents of the UN Conference.)*
(21) *Soviet Union at the San Francisco Conference* (London: "Soviet News," 1945) p. 18.
(22) *Ibid.*
(23) *Radians'ka Ukraina,* April 28, 1945. Official organ of the Central Committee of the Communist Party of Ukraine, of the Supreme Council and the Council of Ministers of the Ukrainian SSR.
(24) *Soviet Union at the San Francisco Conference,* 29-30.
(25) *Ibid.*, 32; the statement of the Belorussian SSR appears on pp. 32-34 of the same pamphlet. The text of the Ukrainian statement appeared in *Radians'ka Ukraina,* April 29, 1945.
(26) *Department of State Bulletin,* XII (305): 806 (April 29, 1945); this letter was released to the press on April 27. See also Harry S. Truman, *Memoirs by Harry S. Truman,* Vol. I: *Year of Decisions* (Garden City: Doubleday, 1955), p. 73.
(27) Vandenberg, 178. Vandenberg wrote in his diary that, when Stettinius asked the delegates to vote on the question of the two Soviet republics, the secretary had combined the vote with the admission of Argentina. The senator also noted that ". . . Nelson Rockefeller (assistant secretary of state for American Republic Affairs) said that the South Americans will insist upon tying the admission of the Argentine into any such deal" (*ibid.*, 177-178). By the "deal" was meant the admission of Ukraine and Belorussia.

It seems that, in order to get an agreement from the Latin American nations to support the Soviet proposal with regard to the two Soviet Union republics, Stettinius had acceded to their demands concerning the admission of one of their sister republics, Argentina, to the world organization (Byrnes, *Speaking Frankly,* 63). The difficulty with Argentina lay in the fact that its government displayed fascist or pro-fascist leanings and was criticized for that by Hull and Roosevelt (Hull, 1400-1401, 1043). At Yalta, Roosevelt seemingly had opposed its admission. *(Yalta Papers,* 773) At San Francisco the American delegation supported Argentina's cause *(Documents of the UN Conference,* (Doc. 42, English), 357-358) which meanwhile had declared war on the Axis in March 1945, while Molotov fought against it, backing his position by quotations from statements of Hull and Roosevelt, rebuking the Farrell regime. However, seeing that Argentina would be admitted in spite of his objections, Molotov then tried to tie this question with the admission of Poland (Lublin government) (*ibid.,* 345-348). The Peruvian delegate, defending Argentina, reproached Molotov by saying that "We voted wholeheartedly for the acceptance of the Ukraine Republic and Byelo-Russian Republic as initial members of the international organization. We had expected that the Soviet Delegation would support the Argentine question" (*ibid.,* 357). As it turned out, Argentina, like the two Soviet Union republics, was admitted, while Poland became a founding member only after the conference was over.

It is interesting that at San Francisco American diplomacy had supported not only the Soviet request for two additional seats, but it did everything possible among the Latin American states to obtain their backing for this proposal. As a result, it had to compromise its position on Argentina. In both cases, United States foreign policy makers made their final moves only after some painful hours of doubt and a considerable amount of reluctance; in both cases, the support given by Washington spelled success; in neither case was any diplomatic advantage gained.

(28) Vandenberg, 180-181. The senator was present at the meeting; about the committee's decision to back the Soviet request, Vandenberg wrote, "(A picture of Anglo-Saxon nations *keeping* faith — altho we all hated what we had to do,)," 181. (Italics and parentheses in the original.)

(29) *Documents of the UN Conference* (Doc. 20, English), 168.

(30) *Ibid.* (Doc. 42, English), 344.

(31) *Pravda,* May 7, 1945; *Radians'ka Ukraina,* May 8, 1945.

(32) See Holub, 30, for some observations on this point.

(33) On Manuilsky's role in the Comintern, see Gunther Nollau, *Die Internationale: Wurzeln und Erscheinungsformen des Proletarischen Internationalismus* (Koln: Verlag fur Politik und Wirtschaft, 1959), and also Kermit E. McKenzie, *Comintern and World Revolution: The Shaping of a Doctrine* (London, New York: Columbia University Press, 1964). A short biographical sketch on Manuilsky may be found in *Bol'shaia Sovetskaia Entsiklopediia,* 2d ed. (Moscow: 1954), Vol. XXVI, 234, and in *Ukrains'ka Radians'ka Entsyklopedia* (Kiev: Akademiia Nauk Ukrains'koi Radians'koi Sotsiialistychnoi Respubliky, 1962), Vol. VIII, 468. The only biography of Manuilsky (very short) is by B. Zavialov, *Dmytro Zakharovych Manuilsky* (Kiev: Vydavnytstvo politychnoi literatury, 1962).

(34) *Radians'ka Ukraina,* May 9, 1945.

(35) *Documents of the UN Conference* (Doc. 55, English), 418.

(36) *Soviet Union at the San Francisco Conference,* 34.

(37) *Ibid.*, 35.

(38) *Ibid.*, 36.

(39) While Manuilsky's observation is essentially true, evidently he disregarded the existence of the Basque and Breton languages.

(40) *Soviet Union at the San Francisco Conference*, 37.

(41) *Ibid.*, 38.

(42) *Ibid.*, 39.

(43) *Ibid.*, 34-39. The text of the commissar's statement in Ukrainian may be found in Ukrains'ka RSR. Ministerstvo Inostranykh Dil. *Ukrains'ka RSR na mizhnarodnii areni; Zbirnyk dokumentiv i materiialiv, 1945-1961* (Kiev: Derzhavne vydavnytstvo politychnoi literatury URSR, 1963), pp. 94-97. The reporters' questions and Manuilsky's answers do not appear here. The memorandum referred to by Manuilsky at the start of the press conference is in *Soviet Union at the San Francisco Conference*, Appendix, 48-62. The Ukrainian text of the memorandum is in *Ukrains'ka RSR na mizhnarodnii areni*, 78-90.

(44) *Radians'ka Ukraina*, August 23, 1945.

(45) Article 110, which deals with "ratification and signature" of the Charter, consists of four paragraphs, the first stipulating that "the present Charter shall be ratified by the signatory states in accordance with their respective constitutional processes."

(46) Byrnes, *Speaking Frankly*, 41-42.

(47) *Ukrains'ka RSR na mizhnarodnii areni*, 4.

PART II
SOVIET DIPLOMACY, UKRAINIAN STYLE

CHAPTER 4
CONCERN OVER COLONIALISM
Champion of Indonesian Independence

This part of the study deals with six political cases which show the major diplomatic activities of the Ukrainian SSR in the United Nations between 1945 and 1950. These activities include 1. issues initiated by the Ukrainian delegation, 2. dicussions in which the delegation of Ukraine sponsored one or more resolutions or submitted amendments to resolutions and 3. questions in which the Ukrainian representatives manifested serious and continuous interest. Only twice did Ukraine initiate a debate: in complaints concerning Indonesia and Greece. In only one case — the Indonesian question — were all three requirements of the "major diplomatic activity" definition met. The Czechoslovak case met only one requirement, and the other four cases each contained two requirements. The stage where significant Ukrainian participation occurred was usually the UN Security Council, at that time the most powerful and influential organ of the United Nations.

The first major diplomatic effort displayed by the Ukrainian SSR in the newly created world organization concerned the political situation in Indonesia. That country, composed of several ethno-linguistic groups (the largest, Javanese) had been ruled in modern times by the Dutch as the Netherlands Indies. Holland had been overrun by the Germans in 1940, and in 1942 the Japanese had seized the Dutch Indies. The Indonesian nationalist movement grew significantly under Japanese occupation, and, in October 1944, Tokyo announced that Indonesia would soon become independent. Japan capitulated to the Allies on August 15, 1945, and two days later Sukarno and Hatta, the Indonesian nationalist leaders, proclaimed their country's independence. On August 18 they became president and vice-president, respectively, of the Republic of Indonesia.

After Japan's unconditional surrender, British Admiral Lord Louis

Mountbatten, Allied commander-in-chief for Southeast Asia, which included the Netherlands Indies, was confronted with several important tasks in that country. One called for British acceptance of the surrender of Japanese troops and the maintenance of order until the Dutch authorities were able to function by themselves. The return of Dutch rule was obviously opposed by the Indonesian nationalists who, meanwhile, tried to organize an army, obtain Japanese weapons, and extend their authority throughout the country. These last two efforts brought the Indonesian Republicans into collision with the Japanese, and fighting ensued. At the end of September British and Allied forces began to arrive, soon followed by small Dutch detachments. The Indonesian nationalists and Dutch troops were each suspicious of the other and armed clashes occurred. Fighting also broke out between the Indonesians and the British, since the latter were generally considered supporters of Dutch colonial rule. The situation became even more tense and complex when British authorities ordered the Japanese troops, whose disarmament was postponed, to recapture some of the cities held by the Indonesians. However, surprised and impressed by the military showing of the Indonesian Republicans, the British put pressure on the Dutch to start negotiations with the nationalists in order to find a solution to the problem. Although talks were held between the parties concerned, no agreement had been reached when the Ukrainian communication of complaint reached the UN Security Council.(1)

In a letter dated January 21, 1946, addressed to the chairman of the Security Council, Manuilsky, head of the Ukrainian delegation, referred to the military actions waged by British and Japanese troops against the Indonesian population. Manuilsky stated that "in the opinion of the Ukrainian Government, this situation created a state of threat to the maintenance of international peace and security, which is covered by Article 34 of the Charter." He concluded his letter by asking the council to investigate the matter and to take necessary steps "to put an end to the present situations."(2)

The Ukrainian complaint was considered at the twelfth meeting of the Security Council on February 7, 1946, held in London. The head of the Ukrainian delegation was invited to take part in the discussion. Invited to make an oral statement supplementing his letter, Manuilsky briefly explained the Ukrainian position. He made some references to the recent past of Indonesia, its occupation by the Japanese, Indonesian resistance to the invaders, and, finally, the surrender of the Japanese troops to the Allies. Manuilsky described how, soon after their surrender, the Japanese, having been authorized to maintain order until the arrival of the British, came into conflict with the population, resulting in disturbances in which heavy arms were used by them against the Indonesian population.

Then, on September 29, 1945, continued the foreign commissar, British and Indian detachments landed in Batavia. The turmoil, however, continued: the British, with the active participation of the Japanese, began military actions against the Indonesians. Supporting his views by quotations from the British press, references to *The New York Times,* and discussions in the House of Commons, Manuilsky then stated that a situation had arisen in Indonesia which endangered international peace and security.

He acknowledged that the presence of the British military forces had the full support of the United Nations, since the purpose of these forces was to accept Japanese surrender. The Ukrainian delegation had no intention of demanding British withdrawal from Indonesia but deemed it wrong to employ the troops to fight a national movement. He expressed surprise that, in the operations directed against the Indonesian people, the British authorities had not hesitated to use Japanese forces. Finally, Manuilsky told his audience, such abnormal conditions could not be tolerated; the Security Council should introduce measures needed to correct the situation. He proposed that a special commission be set up by the council to study the problem and bring peace.(3)

British Secretary of State for Foreign Affairs, Ernest Bevin, observed that, since the Ukrainian delegate did not ask British troops to leave Indonesia, their presence apparently did not constitute a threat to peace and security. He was, therefore, at a loss as to how to answer Manuilsky. Before discussing the matter of whether a special commission should be created to be sent to Indonesia, the British diplomat tried to explain why his country had sent troops to Indonesia and what their task was. He rejected the charges made by Manuilsky and expressed his opposition to sending a commission to Indonesia. Such a commission was not necessary because a conference was in progress to solve the difficulty. If the United Nations wanted to assist in the matter, it could do so by encouraging the negotiators to work hard to achieve a settlement. Bevin concluded his reply by saying that since the Dutch constituted the sovereign power in Indonesia, the question of a commission should be left to their discretion.(4)

This statement seemed to leave the problem of a commission open. When next it was the turn of the Dutch representative, Eelco van Kleffens, to speak, he followed the line taken by his English counterpart. He justified the presence of British troops in what he called a "part of the territory of the Kingdom of the Netherlands" and mentioned their forebearance in the face of the attacks made against them. The Dutch delegate did not identify the Indonesian Nationalist Movement — which to him was legitimate — with the atrocities that had been committed in the country, but blamed them, instead, on terrorists. From the point of view of the United Nations Charter, van Kleffens said, he saw neither dispute nor situation that would endanger international peace and security. He concluded that no case existed for the Security Council to be concerned about. With regard to a commission to be sent to Indonesia, the Dutch spokesman did not take a definite stand.(5)

The first meeting of the Security Council dealing with the Ukrainian complaint concerning the Indonesian situation saw Great Britain, one of the Great Powers which hadhelped Ukraine attain UN membership, bear the brunt of Manuilsky's criticism. A former Comintern leader, now representing the Ukrainian SSR, Manuilsky was now championing Indonesian national aspirations. The British, attacked in their own capital, were evidently annoyed at the charges, and, together with the Dutch, defended British policies.

The debate was continued on February 9 with another supplementary statement by the Ukrainian representative, who pointed out that the discussion thus far, had showed three indisputable points: 1. British troops had been employed to combat the Indonesian people, 2. Japanese troops were engaged in these actions, and 3. none of the facts mentioned had been disproved by the representatives of Great Britain and the Netherlands. After further argumentation with the position taken by the two Western diplomats, Manuilsky formulated his arguments into four proposals. First, he stated that it was neither just nor right for British troops to be used against the Indonesians. Next was the proposal considering it intolerable that Japanese military forces had fought the Indonesian population, which was defending its national rights. Third, Manuilsky insisted that all peoples, according to the UN Charter, possessed rights to decide their own national destiny(6) a right, of course, that should also belong to the Indonesian nation. Last, he proposed that a United Nations commission be dispatched to Indonesia to deal with the matter at hand. After presenting these proposals, the Ukrainian delegate asked Bevin if he could not accept them.(7)

The British diplomat replied by concentrating his attention on whether or not the United Nations had a right to intervene in the domestic matters of states. Quoting the provisions of the Charter, which denied such a right, Bevin voiced his opposition against interfering in the internal affairs of Indonesia under Dutch sovereignty; the Indonesian problem should be dealt with by the Netherlands. "Are we always going, when internal troubles arise," asked Bevin, "to be sending commissions to investigate and deal with the problems arising within a sovereign power?'' He said that he ''cannot agree to it as a question of principle.'' His final advice was that the Security Council should not meedle in a nation's internal affairs.(8) The Dutch Foreign Minister, van Kleffens, who spoke after Bevin, supported the British representative that the United Nations organization could not deal with the domestic matters of any state(9)

The next day, at the fourteenth meeting of the Security Council, the delegate of the USSR, Andrei Y. Vyshinskii, tried to reinforce Manuilsky's arguments. In a lengthy statement the Soviet spokesman vigorously supported the position of the Ukrainian delegation. To him it was imperative that a commission made up of the representatives of the United States, Great Britain, China, the Netherlands, and the Soviet Union be sent to Indonesia. Vyshinskii brushed aside the argument advanced by the English and the Dutch foreign ministers that the United Nations could not intervene, since such a course would infringe on the sovereign rights of the Netherlands. He pointed out that there existed internal matters of states which bordered or even encroached upon international relations, thus endangering the peace and security of the world. In such cases UN intervention would be quite in order.(10)

At the sixteenth meeting, on February 11, Manuilsky, after a brief defense of the merits of his case, asked the members of the Security Council to accept the following proposal:

> After hearing the statement made by the delegation of the Ukrainian SSR on the situation which in Indonesia threatens international peace and security, a situation in which British troops are being used in military action against the National Movement of Liberation, and in which enemy Japanese troops are also being used for the same purpose;
>
> after hearing the statements made by the Foreign Minister of Great Britain, Mr. Bevin, and of the Netherlands, Mr. van Kleffens;
>
> after exchanging views on the question raised, the Security Council decides;
>
> to set up a commission consisting of representatives of the United States, the Soviet Union, China, Great Britain and the Netherlands which should carry out an inquiry on the spot, establish peace in Indonesia, and report to the Security Council on the result of their work.(11)

Just after the proposal was made, a question was raised by the president of the council as to whether the Ukrainian delegate had the right to make a proposal in that body, since Ukraine was not a member of the council. In a discussion on this procedural matter, which consumed most of the session and during which the representatives of Egypt, China, the Netherlands, Poland, France, the Soviet Union, and the United States voiced their views, it was finally agreed that the Ukrainian delegation was so entitled.(12)

The decisive test came in a vote on February 13, at the eighteenth meeting(13) of the Security Council, the last session devoted to the Ukrainian complaint. Manuilsky's resolution was defeated when it received only two votes of the possible eleven when seven were required to obtain council approval.(14) The Indonesian debate, begun by Ukraine, was over.

The diplomatic debut of the Ukrainian SSR in the United Nations was a failure. Manuilsky's arguments, supported by the representative of the Soviet Union, were of no avail against the determined stand of Western diplomacy. In his statements the Ukrainian delegate was rather cautious, and the role of the angry communist crusader was reserved for Vyshinskii. Yet, in the course of the debates the name of Ukraine found its way into the press.(15) It seemed as if the Ukrainian SSR had suddenly begun to play an important role in world politics, starting with a defense of Indonesian liberties.

Several Soviet authors attached considerable importance to the Ukrainian activities in 1946 in the Security Council. Contributors to a Soviet collective work proudly stated that "the Ukrainian SSR was the first to turn the attention of the world community to the events taking place in Indonesia. The whole world then heard in the United Nations Organization the voice of Ukraine in defense of the Indonesian people."(16) Svetlana Krasil'shchikova, author of a work about the UN and national movements of liberation, wrote,

> The appeal of the Ukrainian SSR to the United Nations Organization had an enormous political significance. This was the first case in the history of the UNO, when before one of its main organs — the Security Council — a question linked with the colonial problem was raised . . . The presentation by the Soviet representative of the Indonesian question in the UNO and his unmasking of the colonizers' policies before the world public opinion proved to be a great help to Indonesia.(17)

In more restrained language, the Western scholar Alastair Taylor said substantially the same thing:

> Despite its inconclusive character, the Council's consideration of the Ukrainian complaint had created an important precedent. The newly formed Council had demonstrated that it considered itself

> competent at least to *discuss* a colonial problem in which the military, political and judicial factors were interrelated. As a result, the way had been paved for a further examination of the Indonesian question . . .(18) (Italics in the original.)

Two years later, while serving on the Security Council,(19) Manuilsky again took an active part in debates on Indonesia. This time, of course, Ukraine was not an initiator of the dispute which was alreay in progress.

Between the time of the Ukrainian complaint and early 1948, the situation in Indonesia underwent considerable change. British troops left the country and the Dutch assumed control of much of Indonesia, but the Republic of Indonesia, proclaimed in August 1945, was a force to reckon with. In March 1947 the Lindggadjati agreement was signed between the two parties. According to it, the Republic of Indonesia was recognized as the *de facto* government of Java and Sumatra; both governments would work toward creation of the United States of Indonesia (composed of the Indonesian Republic, the State of Borneo, and the Great Eastern State); and the Netherlands-Indonesian Union under the Queen of the Netherlands would be formed. This agreement failed, however, and in July 1947 the Dutch launched a well-prepared attack against the Indonesian Republic (sometimes called the Dutch First Police Action). The hostilities brought the intervention of the UN Security Council, which called on both sides to cease their military operations and also offered its good offices to settle the conflict. As a result, the Committee of Good Offices came into being and succeeded in bringing representatives of the Netherlands and the Indonesian Republic to the conference table in December 1947. In January 1948 the Ranville agreement, generally favorable to the Dutch, was signed aboard the USN *Ranville*.(20)

On February 20, 1948, Vasyl' Tarasenko, substituting for Manuilsky, hurled accusation after accusation against the Netherlands, the United Kingdom, and the United States. He called them colonizers who desired to exploit and plunder Indonesia. Reminding the members of the Security Council of the Ukrainian proposal of two years ago to dispatch a commission with a purpose to investigate the situation in Indonesia, Tarasenko spared no effort to tell his listeners that the negative decision of the majority on this point had been a big blow to the Indonesian Republic. Charging the Netherlands with aggression and praising the Indonesian government for "a remarkable spirit of conciliation" in its endeavor to achieve a settlement with the Dutch, the Ukrainian diplomat labeled the Committee of Good Offices as the "Committee of Good Offices for the Netherlands Usurpers." The lengthy statement was concluded by an appeal to the Security Council to change its present course of action, "call to order the extremist Netherlands usurpers, and repair the wrong done to the Indonesian people, for which the Security Council itself is largely to blame."(21) No resolution or proposal was suggested, however.

Tarasenko's words were much harsher than Manuilsky's on a similar occasion but cannot be explained by the differences in the two men. When Manuilsky had spoken in February 1946, the Cold War was just beginning, and the hopes of the "Strange Alliance" were not yet extinguished. It is true that there was a chill in Vyshinskii's voice in the beginning of 1946, but the Ukrainian foreign commissar was restrained and his statements were almost tolerable. No such restraint could be seen in the Soviet Ukrainian delegate, Tarasenko, two years later, when the Cold War was in full swing. By this time, too, the enemies of Indonesia had apparently grown in number. Besides criticizing Great Britain, a primary target of the 1946 charges, the attack was directed against the Netherlands, now the primary villain, and also against the United States. Although Washington had played a helpful role procuring UN membership for Ukraine, it found itself criticized by Tarasenko with the old colonial powers helping Dutch imperialism against the Indonesian liberation movement.(22)

On several occasions throughout 1948 the Ukrainian representatives discussed the Indonesian problem in the Security Council. On June 17 Tarasenko attacked the Committee of Good Offices for its neutral report on the situation in Indonesia; he said that the report did not contain "an objective and correct opinion on events, for that would mean condemning the Netherlands Government." The neutral position of the committee was further explained by its unwillingness to admit before the world that the Indonesian people wanted to rid themselves of the Dutch and that the latter continued to suppress Indonesian freedom. The Ukrainian delegate again criticized the actions of Dutch authorities in Indonesia, charging them with a desire to bring back the colonial rule; he also compared the Dutch presence in that country with the occupation of Holland by Hitler's Germany.

> The Dutch people remember the "blessing" they enjoyed under the foreign aggressor. Why, then cannot the Netherlands Government visualize the position of the Indonesian people? What grounds can there be to think that this people looks upon the Netherlands occupation differently from the way in which the people of the Netherlands viewed the Hitlerite occupation?

Tarasenko urged the Security Council to exert more influence on the events occurring in Indonesia and to assist its people. The council must seek a solution to this problem he said, and must not be inactive merely because the Committee of Good Offices was unable to settle the matter.(23)

Two weeks later, on July 1, Manuilsky continued the "hard line" approach in the Indonesian dispute. He began by censuring the trend in international relations to use the services of "committees of good offices." Said the Ukrainian foreign minister,(24)

> The distinguishing characteristic of all the "committees of good offices" is that, no matter what their composition or the number of their members, no matter in what part of the world the dispute takes place, the interests of the United States are invariably represented on them. The decisions of these committees resemble those medicines which do not cure the patient, but merely drive the illness inward, so that it soon flares up again, more violent and dangerous than ever.

From observations on the role of "committees" in general, Manuilsky turned to the particular one in Indonesia. Stating that it was organized at the suggestion of the American delegation, he drew attention to its reports, pointing out that their helpless presentation of the affairs in Indonesia followed "a definite political plan" whose aim was to destroy the Republic of Indonesia. Manuilsky accused the Netherlands and other colonial powers of trying to dismember Indonesia and to set up several local governments which would be weak and easy to control. In such a disunited country there would be no difficulty for foreign monopolies to exploit the natural wealth of the land. The United States, like the Netherlands, was also interested in the fragmentation of Indonesia, he charged; the reason for this lay in the fact that United States "ruling circles" eventually hoped to take the place of the Dutch as the dominant power in the area. That would happen after the so-called Indonesian-Netherlands Union, to be created at the initiative of the Dutch government after the latter, because of its own weakness, had failed to bring about Indonesia's dismemberment. It was quite obvious, Manuilsky further observed, that Soviet delegations did not support the imperialistic designs other governments harbored against Indonesia. Referring to the Ukrainian letter of January 1946, which had been the starting point of the debates, the foreign minister noted that only the delegation of the Soviet Union had expressed support for it. And yet "the course of events has proved that the Soviet delegations were right, and those who in January 1946 caused their proposals to be rejected, bear the blame for the blood which has been, and is being shed in Indonesia.'' Manuilsky concluded by saying that ''the delegation of the Ukrainian SSR has supported, and will continue to support, every measure intended to achieve genuine independence of the Indonesian people, the integrity of their territory and the establishment of a democratic state.''(25)

On both these occasions no concrete measure was suggested by the Ukrainian delegate on how to deal with the situation in Indonesia. However, in Paris, on December 27, Tarasenko submitted a resolution. Following an established practice of the Ukrainian delegation, he reminded the Security Council of the initiative of the Ukrainian SSR in 1946 which had drawn attention to the Indonesian question. Following still another practice, he accused the United States of fostering Dutch aggression against the Indonesian people. ''It remains a fact,'' said the Communist diplomat, ''that without the economic, financial and political aid of the United States of America, the Netherlands would not have been in a position to carry on its aggressive policy in Indonesia for more than three years.'' Blaming the majority of the Security Council for the recent events,(26) and again emphasizing American responsibility for what was happening in Indonesia, Tarasenko observed that both Soviet delegations had tried in vain to warn the members of the council of ''inescapable consequences'' that would ensue from their support for the Netherlands government. Now the consequence was visible: the Dutch had attacked the Indonesian Republic — ''An attack which in its treachery competes with similar deeds of Hitlerite Germany.''

After criticizing the Security Council for adopting the resolution on December 24 in regard to the cessation of hostilities in Indonesia,(27) which he thought was too lenient to the Netherlands, the Ukrainian representative was ready to propose his own resolution:

> *The Security Council*
> *Considers it necessary* that the Netherlands troops should be withdrawn immediately to the position which they occupied before military operations against the Indonesian Republic were renewed.(28)

In the course of the discussion that followed Tarasenko's remarks, several speakers took the floor, including the representative of the Soviet Union, Yakov Malik, who proposed another resolution(29) and also urged the Security Council to support the Ukrainian proposal.(30) However, both draft resolutions were defeated.(31)

On December 29 the Ukrainian delegate voiced dissatisfaction over the rejection of the Soviet proposals. Repeating some of his earlier charges against the Netherlands and the United States, Tarasenko wondered why the Security Council had rejected the resolution put forth by the USSR and the Ukrainian SSR.

> Why did the Security Council — or rather its majority — take such a course? There is only one unavoidable conclusion — it did so because it is opposed to the freedom and independence not only of the people of Indonesia, but the peoples of Asia and the Far East in general. It is giving the Netherlands aggressor every opportunity to destroy the Indonesian Republic.(32)

These activities during 1948 of the Ukrainian delegation showed that the Ukrainian SSR supported the Republic of Indonesia completely. Always working in unison with the USSR, Ukraine displayed an unwavering concern over the fate of the newly created Indonesian state. The records of the Security Council make it clear that the Ukrainian representatives, together with the spokesmen for the Soviet Union, acted much more belligerently in defense of Indonesia than did the representatives of the Republic of Indonesia who had been invited to state their case. Such a posture looks familiar to students of Soviet foreign policy when one remembers that, on an earlier occasion, Foreign Commissar George Chicherin proved to be "more Turkish than the Turks."(33) But where Chicherin's purpose was clear, the same cannot be said of Soviet intentions in the Indonesian dispute. Speaking only about the actions of the Soviet Ukrainian delegation, at least three political goals can be discerned.

First, the Ukrainian representatives tried to create an image — in Asia and worldwide — that they were the champions of awakened nationalism, anti-colonialism, and anti-imperialism. In pursuing the steady course of unconditional support for the Indonesian nationalist movement, which was anti-Dutch and therefore anti-colonial and anti-imperialist, the Ukrainian arguments were meant to convince the world that Soviet policies were on the side of peoples struggling for their independence. Second, in attacking the Netherlands, which found itself in an embarrassing and untenable position, the Ukrainian delegate took aim at discrediting not only Dutch colonialism, but all Western colonialism in general. And third, since there existed some grounds for thinking that the United States position was pro-Dutch,(34) a concerted effort was made by the Ukrainian SSR to picture American policies as pro-colonial and hostile to the emerging forces of nationalism and to independence movements. This last effort, of course, fitted well with the prevailing atmosphere of the Cold War.

During the course of United Nations debates on Indonesia in 1948,

Ukraine again showed an active interest in the matter. The position of the Ukrainian delegation was basically unchanged; it was still thoroughly anti-Dutch, and the attacks on the United States and the United Kingdom lost none of their disagreeable qualities. The defense of the Indonesian Republic continued as before, although some Indonesians were now subject to harsh criticism.

At the 403rd meeting of the Security Council, held at Lake Success, Tarasenko expressed his differences with the joint draft resolution submitted at the previous meeting.(35) He sought to stress four points. First he opposed the resolution's provision which endeavored to stop guerrilla activities against the Dutch forces. The Ukrainian diplomat insisted that

> guerrilla warfare against an invading foe has always been a legitimate means of defense for an invaded nation. It was considered so in the case of Spanish guerilla forces striking at Napoleon's armies. It was considered so when the partisans of all occupied countries in Europe prosecuted that war against the Hitlerite aggressor and thus helped in the defeat of Nazi Germany. The guerrilla warfare waged by the Indonesian people against the Netherlands aggressor which has occupied the Indonesian Republic, is the same legitimate fight.

Tarasenko also voiced his displeasure at the authorization of a UN commission to observe elections in Indonesia, because Dutch troops were still occupying the Indonesian Republic and it was impossible to have "free elections of any kind without the prior withdrawal of the Netherlands occupation forces." Further, he was quite skeptical about the recommendation for the establishment of a provisional government in Indonesia, for it would mean that it would be composed of pro-Dutch collaborationists. Obviously, "a government set up in such circumstances could not possibly prepare the way for a truly independent Indonesian government." Finally, he objected to the provision that would retain Dutch troops to help keep law and order in the country on the grounds that they were committing atrocities against the population.(36)

The slightly amended joint draft resolution was adopted on January 28, 1949.(37) The Security Council did not discuss the Indonesian question again until March 10.(38) On March 16 the Ukrainian representative resumed a by-now familiar line of reasoning. This time Tarasenko attacked the Dutch not only for their performances vis-a-vis the decisions of the Security Council but also for their future plans to have a round table conference at The Hague to settle the Indonesian problem. Referring to the January 28 resolution, he accused the Netherlands of disregarding its provisions:

> The call made in the Security Council resolution for the release of the arrested leaders of the Indonesian Republic, as also the demand for the immediate cessation of all military operations against the Republic by the Netherlands Government, is a voice crying in the wilderness.

Labeling the effort to organize a round table conference a farce, and registering his surprise that the United Nations commission did not turn down the Dutch government's invitation to attend it (without even consulting the council), the Ukrainian diplomat stated that the real task of this conference was to find "an appropriate way to destroy the Indonesian Republic and restore the old order in Indonesia." The Dutch endeavor to create the United States of Indonesia was explained as an attempt "to set up a puppet state with a puppet government having illusory sovereignty and illusory power." Expressing his regret over the fact that the Ukrainian resolution of December 1948, which would have contributed to the settlement of the problem, had been rejected because of the opposition from the United States and the United Kingdom, Tarasenko said that the discussion on Indonesia had become a mockery.(39)

On December 3, the Ad Hoc Political Committee of the fourth session of the General Assembly again took up the Indonesian question, completing its discussion on the same day. Manuilsky, the Ukrainian representative displayed a keen interest in what seemed to be an unending debate on this matter and the polemic continued as lively as ever.

Manuilsky objected to the joint draft resolution submitted by the Indian delegate(40) and proposed a resolution of his own. The Ukrainian resolution proposed that the General Assembly request the Dutch to withdraw their troops to the line they held before the hostilities started in December 1948, require the Dutch to "release the Indonesian political prisoners and put an end to the campaign of terror against the Indonesian people," and ". . . propose the establishment of a United Nations commission composed of representatives of the states, members of the Security Council," whose task would be to watch over the Netherlands authorities implementing the above provisions and to carry out the investigation of brutalities by the Dutch against "the democratic leaders of the Indonesian people." It also urged the Assembly "to instruct the commission to prepare, and submit to the Security Council within three months, proposals for the settlement of the conflict . . . on the basis of the recognition of the independence and sovereign rights of the Indonesian people,'' and also ''to dissolve the United Nations Commission for Indonesia.''(41)

Alluding to the joint resolution, Manuilsky said that the Ad Hoc Political Committee could not endorse The Hague agreement since the documents of the Round Table Conference were not yet sufficiently circulated. He challenged the Dutch statement, made at the plenary meeting of the General Assembly,(42) that, as a result of The Hague negotiations, the Indonesians would enjoy peace, and he further charged that Dutch agression was still a reality, abetted by the United Kingdom and the United States. Criticizing the Hatta government which had signed the agreement with the Dutch, he pointed out that it did not represent the Republic of Indonesia and that it was opposed by some parts of the Republican Army. The ''democratic circles'' opposed both the Hatta government and The Hague decisions. A proclamation had been issued ''by the leaders of the patriotic movement'' in Java, stating that the Indonesians would not accede to The Hague agreement. After all, such an accord ''between the Dutch aggressors and the Hatta clique deprived the Indonesian people of its sovereign right to be independent; it did not allow them to enter into diplomatic relations with other states . . .'' Expressing doubt as to the validity of the Dutch promise to withdraw their armed forces from Indonesia, Manuilsky said that the United Nations could not believe this promise; the ''repeated breaches of faith and violations of the Security Council decisions'' by the Netherlands did not warrant it. Such ''breaches of faith'' had resulted in the territorial shrinking of the Republic of Indonesia, which would thus become ''one of the sixteen states forming the so-called United States of Indonesia, the other fifteen being the artificial creations of the Netherlands Government headed by puppet governments similar to the Hatta clique.''

The majority of the committee did not share the views of the Ukrainian SSR representative and expressed satisfaction with the results of the Round Table Conference, thus supporting the joint draft resolution. The representatives of the Soviet Union and Poland, however voiced their approval of the Ukrainian proposal and their disapproval of the joint resolution. To the Soviet delegate, the settlement reached at The Hague constituted a clear betrayal of the Indonesian people, and the betrayers were the ''Hatta and Sukarno clique.'' The Polish delegate, too, used some strong language in condemning the agreement. Finally, when after some procedural clashes the joint draft resolution was put to the vote, it obtained an easy victory, while the Ukrainian proposal met defeat without being voted upon.(43)

The battle now shifted to the General Assembly, where on December

7 the discussion revolved around the Ad Hoc Political Committee's work on the Indonesian question. The battle was fought with familiar weapons on familiar grounds. Manuilsky and the representatives of the USSR, Poland, the the Belorussian SSR argued that the General Assembly should not adopt the joint draft resolution passed by the majority of the committee; instead, they favored the proposal of the Ukrainian SSR and urged its acceptance. The opposite viewpoint was expressed by the supporters of the joint resolution, which in the end prevailed over the views of the communist delegates. The performance of the Ad Hoc Political Committee with regard to the two resolutions was repeated in the General Assembly.(44)

The stormy dispute over the Indonesian problem, however, continued on December 12 and 13 in the Security Council. Again two resolutions were submitted — one by Canada and the other by Ukraine. In tone and content the Canadian proposal resembled the joint resolution adopted by the General Assembly; the proposal of the Ukrainian delegation was identical to the one rejected by both the Ad Hoc Political Committee and the General Assembly. In the ensuing debate, the Ukrainian representative, this time Andrii Halahan, delivered perhaps the longest speech ever made by a Ukrainian delegate at any session of the Security Council on Indonesia. He repeated what his colleagues Manuilsky and Tarasenko had said, and, as if sadly conscious that the days of the Ukrainian SSR in the Security Council were numbered, he spoke at some length again at the next meeting, dwelling on the virtues of the Ukrainian resolution. As on the two previous occasions, the proposal was not adopted. Because of the veto power of the Soviet Union, however, the Canadian resolution was also defeated.(45)

In its continued and unflinching defense of Indonesian sovereignty, the delegation of the Ukrainian SSR, as the December 1949 debates show, assailed not only the Dutch and other Western governments, but also the government of the Indonesian Republic under Prime Minister Hatta. Was the delegation attacking the very thing it had so long defended? Had there been a change of policy? Not at all; the Soviet policy makers were against any Netherlands-Indonesian compromise short of the total withdrawal of the Dutch from Indonesia, and any agreement between the Netherlands and the Hatta governments which stopped short of this goal was to be discredited, together with those working for it. It is curious that in order to prove that Indonesia was allegedly being deprived of its independence as a result of the negotiations at The Hague, Manuilsky pointed to Indonesia's lack of diplomatic relations with foreign countries. Irrespective of the truth of this statement, did the Ukrainian overlook his own political backyard? Did he tend to ignore the fact that, at the time he spoke, the country he represented in the UN also had no relations with foreign states? There were no embassies in Kiev nor were there Ukrainian embassies in any foreign capital.(46) Perhaps the difference between Indonesia and Ukraine was that the latter had a *right* to establish diplomatic relations but had chosen not to exercise such an elementary prerogative of statehood — a strange way, indeed, of displaying its sovereignty.

Footnotes

(1) See Charles Wolf, Jr., *Indonesian Story: The Birth, Growth and Structure of the Indonesian Republic* (New York: John Day, 1948); George McThurman Kahin, *Nationalism and Revolution in Indonesia* (Ithaca, N.Y.: Cornell University Press, 1952); Leslie H. Palmier, *Indonesia and the Dutch* (London: Oxford University Press, 1962).

(2) United Nations, Security Council, *Journal of the Security Council,* First Year, No. 2, January 24, 1946 (London, 1946), p. 15 (hereafter cited as Security Council, *Journal).* Article 34 stipulates that "the Security Council may investigate any dispute, or any situation which may lead to international friction or give rise to a dispute, in order to determine whether the continuance of the dispute or the situation is likely to endanger the maintenance of international peace and security." In his letter, Manuilsky also mentioned Article 35 (1) which reads: "Any Member of the United Nations may bring any dispute, or any situation of the nature referred to in Article 34, to the attention of the Security Council or of the General Assembly."

(3) Security Council, *Journal,* No. 10, February 13, 1946, 179-182. The Ukrainian text of Manuilsky's statement appeared in *Radians'ka Ukraina,* February 9, 1946.

(4) *Ibid.,* 182-186. Apparently, by "conference," Bevin was referring to the negotiations that were being held between the Dutch and the Indonesians at the time the Ukrainian complaint was being discussed in the Security Council.

(5) *Ibid.,* 186-189.

(6) In all probability, Manuilsky was referring to that section of the Charter, Chapter I, Article 1 (2), which states that one of the aims of the UN is "To develop friendly relations among nations based on respect for the principle of equal rights and self-determination of peoples . . ."

(7) Security Council, *Journal,* No. 11, February 15, 1946, 192-197. At one point, Manuilsky, in referring to the remarks made by Bevin and van Kleffens at the previous meeting, said that "the soldiers of my country do not fight to defend the interests of Shell Oil. They fight in order to defend their country" (*ibid.,* 194). James Reston, who covered the proceedings, wrote: "like a good-natured schoolmaster lecturing to his class, Mr. Manuilsky calmly . . . sought to show that the British Army was fighting against downtrodden Indonesians in the interests of the Shell Oil Company" (see *The New York Times,* Feburary 10, 1946, p. 25).

(8) Security Council, *Journal,* No. 11, 197-199. In his polemic with the communist diplomat, Bevin, in citing the efforts of the Dutch to settle their differences with the Indonesians, said that "the best advice you can give the Indonesians is: there is Dr. van Mook, who is the responsible representative of the Netherlands, ready and waiting with proposals which, if I understand constitutions and rights at all, go as far as anything I have seen; certainly, I think, as far as any rights that the Ukrainian Government has within the Soviet Union" (*ibid.,* 197).

(9) *Ibid.,* 199-201.

(10) *Ibid.,* 201-210. Vyshinskii's performance at the Security Council drew this reaction from correspondent Reston: "Taking up the attack where the Ukrainian Foreign Minister, Dimitri Manuilsky, had left off, but, abandoning Mr. Manuilsky's efforts at sweet reasonabless, Andrei Y. Vishinskii, Soviet Vice Foreign Commissar, suddenly adopted the role of grand inquisitor . . . Indeed, there was scarcely any charge that Mr. Vishinsky did not level at the British and the Dutch either by direct statement or oblique innuendo during the two hours he held the floor. By comparison, Mr. Manuilsky's statements were downright complimentary" (see *The New York Times,* February 11, 1946, p. 1).

(11) Security Council, *Journal,* No. 13, February 19, 1946, 221-223.

(12) *Ibid.,* 223-230.

(13) At the seventeenth session, demanding a decision with regard to the Ukrainian proposition, Manuilsky said that "the Security Council cannot afford to follow the example of Pontius Pilate, who, we are told, decided to wash his hands of the wrong which had taken place" (see *ibid.,* 243).

(14) Security Council, *Journal,* No. 14, February 20, 1946, 251-252. The resolution was supported by the USSR and Poland.

(15) The Western press regarded the moves of the Ukrainian delegation in the Security Council as just another manifestation of Moscow's diplomacy.

(16) Ukrainian SSR, Akademiia Nauk, Institut Istorii, *Ukrains'kaia SSR i zarubezhnye sotsialisticheskie strany* (Kiev: Izdatel'stvo "Naukova Dumka," 1965), p. 102.

(17) S. A. Krasil'shchikova, *OON i natsional'no-osvoboditel'noe dvizhenie* (Moscow: Izdatel'stvo "Mezhdunarodnye otnosheniia," 1964), pp. 25-26.)

(18) Alastair May Taylor, *Indonesian Independence and the United Nations* (Ithaca: Cornell University Press, 1960), p. 43.

(19) The Ukrainian SSR was elected as a nonpermanent member of the Security Council on November 13, 1947, by the General Assembly on the twelfth ballot, for a period of two years from January 1, 1948, to December 31, 1949. See *Yearbook of the United Nations, 1947-1948* (New York: Lake Success, 1949), pp. 30-31, 337 (hereafter cited as *Yearbook).*

(20) See Kahin, *Nationalism and the Revolution in Indonesia,* and Palmier, *Indonesia and the Dutch.*

(21) United Nations, Security Council, *Official Records,* Third Year (New York: Lake Success), Nos. 16-35, 251st meeting, February 20, 1948, pp. 227-236 (hereafter cited as Security Council, *Records).*

(22) *Ibid.,* 231, 232, 233.

(23) Security Council, *Records,* Third Year, No. 86, 323rd meeting, June 17, 1948, 40-46. Tarasenko, following Manuilsky's remark made in 1946, said that the Security Council "cannot remain aloof and, like Pontius Pilate,

wash its hands of the matter" (*ibid.*, 46).

(24) Formerly, the foreign commissar. On March 15, 1946, the Council of People's Commissars of the USSR and the Councils of People's Commissars of the Union and the Autonomous Republics were reorganized by the Supreme Soviet of the USSR into the Council of Ministers of the USSR and the Councils of Ministers of the Union and the Autonomous Republics (see *Istoriia Sovetskoi Konstitiutsii: Sbornik dokumentov 1917-1957*, 410-411).

(25) United Nations, Security Council, *Official Records*, Third Year, No. 91, 328th meeting, July 1, 1948, pp. 10-14. It should be stated that, besides the USSR, the Ukrainian position in 1946 was supported by the delegate from Poland; Manuilsky did not mention this in his statement.

(26) "On 19 December 1948 the Dutch bombed the airfield at Jogjakarta, and so began their Second Police Action. They quickly captured Sukarno, Hatta, Sjahrir and half of the Republican Cabinet . . . During the next week the Dutch seized the principal remaining Republican-held cities of both Java and Sumatra" (see Palmier, 65-66).

(27) The resolution, in part said that "The Security Council, *noting* with concern the resumption of hostilities in Indonesia and *having* taken note of the reports of the Committee of Good Offices, *calls upon* the parties (a) to cease hostiliites forewith and (b) immediately to release the President and the political prisoners . . ." (see *Yearbook*, 1948-1949, 216).

(28) Security Council, *Records*, Third Year, No. 135, 383rd meeting, December 27, 1948, 3-7.

(29) *Ibid.*, 8. The USSR proposal called on the Security Council to order the Netherlands to stop its hostilities against the Indonesian Republic "within twenty-four hours of the adoption of the present resolution."

(30) *Ibid.*, 32.

(31) *Ibid.*, 35.

(32) Security Council, *Records*, Third Year, No. 137, 396th meeting, December 29, 1948, 44-46.

(33) See Louis Fischer, *The Soviets in World Affairs: A History of the Relations between the Soviet Union and the Rest of the World, 1917-1929* (Princeton: Princeton University Press, 1951), Vol. I, p. 404.

(34) Alastair Taylor pointed out that examination of the Security Council debates indicates that "the juridical arguments advanced by the United States delegation together with the political techniques which it was chiefly responsible for having the Council adopt did in fact work consistently to the advantage of the Netherlands between August 1947 and December 1948." The author maintained that this position "stemmed not so much from an avowed pro-Dutch policy as from the consequences of an over-all foreign policy which, . . . felt compelled by its assessment of the Cold War to give top priority to strengthening Western Europe — with the inevitable advantages that thereby accrued to the Netherlands." Taylor observed, however, that in January 1949, there occurred a basic change of United States policy concerning the Indonesian problem, caused by various pressures outside the Council (Taylor, 398-399).

(35) This lengthy resolution proposed by China, Cuba, Norway, and the United States on January 21, called upon both the Dutch and the Indonesians to stop military operations; called upon the Netherlands to free the political prisoners; recommended the formation of a temporary federal government, the holding of elections to a constituent assembly and the transfer of sovereignty

from the Netherlands to the United States of Indonesia; and suggested the establishment of the United Nations Commission for Indonesia which would replace the Committee of Good Offices and which would have wider powers than the latter. (see Security Council, *Records,* Fourth Year, Supplements for January 1949 (Doc. S/1219), 53-56.

(36) Security Council, *Records,* Fourth Year, No. 7, 403rd meeting, January 25, 1949, 17-20.

(37) Security Council, *Records,* Fourth Year, No. 9, 406th meeting, January 28, 1949, 19-33.

(38) See *Yearbook,* 1948-1949, 223.

(39) Security Council, *Records,* Fourth Year, No. 22, 419th meeting, March 16, 1949, 25-28.

(40) This resolution, sponsored by several states, proposed that the General Assembly should (1) welcome the accord reached at the Round Table Conference at The Hague; (2) commend both parties as well as the UN Commission for Indonesia for their work; and (3) welcome "the forthcoming establishment of the Republic of the United States of Indonesia as an independent, sovereign state"; see United Nations, General Assembly, *Ad Hoc Political Committee, Official Records of the Fourth Session of the General Assembly, Annex to the Summary Records of Meetings,* Vol. I, 1949 (Lake Success, New York: 1949), p. 65 (Doc. A/AC.31/L.50) (hereafter cited as *Ad Hoc Political Committee).*

The Hague conference, attended by representatives of the Netherlands, the Republic of Indonesia, and other parts of Indonesia not included in the Republic, as well as by the United Nations Commission for Indonesia, lasted from August 23 to November 2, 1949. The conference resulted in several agreements. The first the Transfer of Sovereignty, said, in part, that "the Kingdom of the Netherlands unconditionally and irrevocably transfers complete sovereignty over Indonesia to the Republic of the United States of Indonesia. . . . The transfer of sovereignty shall take place at the latest on 30 December 1949." The second agreement, the United Statute, stipulated the creation of the Netherlands-Indonesian Union and the future cooperation between the two equal and completely independent partners. The third document, the Agreement on Transitional Measures, concerned itself, *inter alia,* with the legal transfer of Indonesia's rights and obligations to the Republic of the United States of Indonesia. This document also contained a special agreement for the gradual withdrawal of the Dutch military forces (*Yearbook,* 1948-1949, 229-233; see also Kahin, 433-445).

(41) *Ad Hoc Political Committee, Annex,* 65 (Doc. A/AC.31/L.51).

(42) United Nations, General Assembly, *Official Records,* Fourth Session (New York: Lake Success), 238th plenary meeting, November 2, 1949, 172-173 (hereafter cited as General Assembly, *Records,* Fourth Session).

(43) United Nations, General Assembly, *Ad Hoc Political Commitee, Official Records of the Fourth Session of the General Assembly* (Lake Success, New York: 1949), 56th meeting, December 3, 1949, 330-339. The majority of the committee decided that the Ukrainian resolution constituted a recommendation to the General Assembly. According to Article 12 (1) of the UN Charter, "while the Security Council is exercising in respect of any dispute or situation the functions assigned to it in the present Charter, the General Assembly shall not make any recommendation with regard to that dispute or situation unless the Security Council so requests." Since the Security Council

was dealing with the Indonesian question, the Ukrainian proposal was not even put to a vote.

(44) General Assembly, *Records,* Fourth Session, 271st and 272nd meetings, December 7, 1949, 550-564. The representative of Belgium, apparently annoyed by the criticisms of the Ukrainian and Belorussian delegations that The Hague agreement meant the betrayal of Indonesian sovereignty, said that these charges were made by the people who "represented precisely populations which did not enjoy any of the fundamental prerogatives of a sovereign State and which certainly enjoyed fewer of such prerogatives than any dependent territory" (*ibid.,* 563).

(45) Security Council, *Records,* Fourth Year, No. 51, 455th meeting, December 12, 1949, 1-32; Security Council, *Records,* Fourth Year, No. 52, 456th meeting, December 13, 1949, 1-38. The full text of the Canadian proposal may be found in Security Council, *Records,* Fourth Year, Supplement for September, October, November and December 1949 (Doc. S/1431), 13-14.

(46) A situation still existing today.

CHAPTER 5
INTEREST IN THE EASTERN MEDITERRANEAN
Enemy of Royalist Greece

Another major interest of the Ukrainian SSR in its political activity within the United Nations related to Greece. This Balkan country was overrun by German troops in 1941, which, together with Italian (until 1943) and Bulgarian forces, constituted the Axis occupation authorities. During Occupation, various guerrilla bands had appeared in Greece, among them the ELAS (National Popular Liberation Army), a military arm of EAM (National Liberation Front). The latter was organized by the Greek Communist Party and comprised several socialist parties and organizations. ELAS, controlled and led by the communists, was the strongest of all Greek guerrillas. In 1943, while the Germans were still in control of the country, ELAS began military activities again other Greek partisans with the obvious intention of becoming the only military power in the land after Axis withdrawal. The Germans left Greece in the fall of 1944, and were followed immediately by the landing of a small British force. With the coming of the British also came the Papandreou government, which was soon opposed by EAM ELAS. In December, the communists, who controlled most of the countryside and drew some sympathy from among the population, decided to overthrow the Papandreou regime and seize power. However, because the Greek government had the support of the British troops (which were later reinforced), it was able to frustrate the communist design.

The communist uprising occurred some two months after an unusual agreement was concluded between Churchill and Stalin in Mowcow that concerned the political fate of some East European and Balkan countries. According to this agreement, which had been ''settled in no more time than it takes to set down'' (to use Churchill's own vivid expression), Rumania, for example, was to be 90 percent under the Russian dominance and 10 percent under ''the others'' — apparently Great Britain and the United States. The sphere of influence in Greece was to be the reverse: 90 percent under British dominance (with consent of the United States) and 10 percent under Russia.(1) In spite of this arrangement, the Greek communists made a bid to seize power. Existing documentary evidence is not sufficent to ascertain whether Stalin had induced or encouraged such an attempt, but there is little doubt that the Greek Communist Party did not embark on the December venture without his knowledge.(2)

The Greek communists were defeated but not destroyed. The Greek Communist Party was allowed by the government to legally participate in the political life of the country; nevertheless, many prominent communists went underground to wait for "another round" in their quest for power. In March 1946, with American, British, and French observers present, elections resulting in a big victory for the non-communist parties were held; the communists had abstained from the elections. Meanwhile, sporadic fighting developed between newly reconstituted communist insurgents and government forces. The Soviet Union, secure in most parts of the Balkans, was pushing toward the eastern Mediterranean. Yugoslavia, Bulgaria, and Albania were now communist-controlled, and clandestine aid for Greek Communist Party guerrillas was expected from them. The Cold War was emerging, British troops could not stay in Greece indefinitely, and the unstable conditions in the country presented an obvious opportunity for the communist leadership to redress its past defeats: civil war was again in the making. When, as a result of the Ukrainian complain, the Security Council was ready to discuss the Greek situation, the plebiscite of September 1, which decided the form of government in Greece, had already been held. About 70 percent of the voters opted for the return of the monarchy. This percentage, together with the gradual strengthening of royalist and right-wing groups as well as persecution of the communists and their sympathizers, could not but convince the Greek Communist Party that its time for striking a victorious blow was running out.(3)

In a telegram of August 24, 1946, addressed to Secretary-General Lie of the UN, the Ukrainian foreign minister directed the attention of the Security Council to what he considered a dangerous situation in the Balkans which threatened "peace and security in this part of Europe. . . ." The reason for such a state of affairs lay in the "irresponsible policy" of the government of Greece in its military aggression against Albania. These activities, according to Manuilsky, were meant to provoke a conflict between the two countries "which would serve as a pretext for the wresting of the southern part of Albania in favour of Greece." The situation was not made any more tolerable by the statement of the Greek authorities that a war existed between Greece and Albania. After accusing the Greek regime of persecuting national minorities in Thrace, Macedonia, and Epirus, the telegram said that

> the principal factor conducive to the situation in the Balkans, as created by this policy of the present Greek Government, is the presence of British troops in Greece and the direct intervention of

> British military representatives in the internal affairs of this Allied country in behalf of aggressive monarchist elements, especially in the preparation of the referendum of 1 September 1946 which is to determine the form of government in Greece.

Manuilsky insisted that to have a referendum in the country, occupied by foreign troops supporting the elements who had sided with Germany and Italy during the war, constituted a violation of Allied war aims as well as of the UN Charter (especially Article 1 (2) which states that every nation has a right to self-determination). Manuilsky maintained that the presence of British troops precluded the validity of such a referendum. In view of these developments, and again, invoking Articles 34 and 35 (1), of the Charter as in the case of Indonesia, the Ukrainian delegate asked the Security Council to place the matter on its agenda.(4)

It was briefly considered on August 28. A dispute immediately ensued between representatives of the Netherlands and the United Kingdom on one hand, and the delegate of the Soviet Union on the other. Both Western diplomats demanded that the Ukrainian complaint be rewritten so that it would substantiate the charges made; otherwise, they argued, it should not be placed on the agenda. Gromyko disagreed; he retorted that the Ukrainian statement should be examined by the Security Council in the form presented. Ridiculing his opponents, he wondered how it was possible to determine whether the Ukrainian document contained the necessary facts without first investigating it. He urged the Security Council to examine the question raised by Ukraine.(5) After lengthy debate on September 3, a vote was taken on whether to include Manuilsky's telegram in the agenda, and the motion was adopted.(6)

On the following day the Ukrainian representative presented his case. Manuilsky observed that the Greek question was not new to the Security Council, for in February 1946, the Soviet Union had drawn its attention to "the terror prevailing in Greece against the democratic forces of the Greek people." Referring to the elections of March 31, 1946, which he attacked as having been rigged, Manuilsky charged the Greek government with the "monarchisation of the country" by having purged "the government organizations and the army (of) republican elements and their replacement by monarchistic elements." He then asserted that the plebiscite of September 1 was not secret because, as the world press reported, transparent envelopes were used in the voting. "In any democratic country that would constitute a reason for annulling the plebiscite, but in Greece, even transparent things visible to the whole world do not worry the present Greek government.'' The polemic against the September plebiscite was supported by a quotation from the American newspaper *PM*(7) of September 3, which Manuilsky read from:

> In 1935, John Theotokis organized a plebiscite in which His Majesty won 97.5 per cent. A colleague of Theotokis told the King candidly: ''Your Majesty, the results are really faked. The real percentage is somewhere about 25 per cent. Nevertheless, we want you back.'' Incidentally, it is the same Theotokis, now Minister of the Interior under the Fascist Government, who cooked up the present plebiscite.

He then turned to what he regarded as the most significant part of his speech. Readily implying that a plebiscite was, in general, an internal matter, Manuilsky pointed out that the plebiscite in question could not really be considered as such in this case for two reasons: the ''prolonged intervention'' of the British in the domestic affairs of this country, violating Article 2 (7) of the UN Charter,(8) and the use of the plebiscite by the Greek government as a tool of aggressive designs against neighboring countries. ''Even today,'' said Manuilsky, ''the Greek Government is demanding the dismemberment of Albania and claiming that one-third of Albanian territory should be ceded to Greece.'' Because of this, the intensification of incidents on the Greco-Albanian border and also on the frontier with Yugoslavia constituted a threat to the peace and security of the Balkan peoples, a matter which could not be ignored by the Security Council.(9)

Within a six-month period the Ukrainian delegation lodged two complaints in the Security Council, and in each case Western (or pro-Western) countries, particularly Great Britain, were the target of its attack. Was there a plan to discredit and thus weaken the West? The behavior of Manuilsky, the top communist dignitary, left no doubt about Soviet intentions, and the chief diplomats of the United States and Great Britain came to regret their past acquiescence in the admission of Ukraine to the UN. Now the dire implications of the Yalta and San Francisco decisions became clear. Since there was no way of revising the situation, however, the only thing left to do was to accept the verbal barrages as gracefully as possible and to prepare some sort of defense.(10)

The Greek reply came on September 5. The representative of Greece, Vassili Dendramis, denied that his country was menacing peace in the Balkans. The danger did not emanate from Greece, but rather from Bulgaria, Yugoslavia, and Albania, all of which maintained larger military forces. Manuilsky's assertion that British troops were interfering in the internal affairs of Greece was not true; they had been requested by the Greek government and remained in Greece with the free consent of the people, who understood that their presence was needed for national security. Dendramis also defended the elections of March 31 and the plebiscite of September 1, and then he accused the Greek Communist Party of fomenting trouble with a view to seizing power. He attacked the Yugoslav press for conducting a "slanderous campaign" against Greece by describing it as a fascist state. Finally, he told Manuilsky that, if he really desired peace in the Balkans, he should give advice to the "proper quarters" and his wish would be satisfied.(11)

In the general discussion that followed this speech, Sir Alexander Cadogan also challenged Manuilsky's views. He ridiculed Manuilsky's interpretation of Article 2(7) of the UN Charter, stating that Paragraph 7 did not deny to any member of the United Nations the right to have its troops on the territory of another member, if the latter had asked for them. He said that the Ukrainian case against the policies of the British government in Greece was entirely unconvincing.(12)

On the same day the Albanian government asked the Security Council to allow it to make a statement on the Balkan situation. Its request was accepted, and on September 9 the Albanian representative, Colonel Tuk Jakova accused the Greek government of constant provocations on the Albanian frontier. He also charged the Greek authorities with "barbarous acts" directed against the Albanian minority and with the imperialist aim of seizing the southern part of his country. Colonel Jakova urged the Security Council to demand of the Greek government cessation of hostile acts toward Albania and toward the Albanian minority in Greece.(13)

The Ukrainian representative spoke again on September 10, criticizing several speakers, including Dendramis and Cadogan, for their negative reactions to his original statement. Manuilsky also defended the Greek communists by stressing the fact that

> it is time to get rid of the legend of the communists as a little bunch of men who have no influence among their own people. The popular masses in all countries scrutinized the communists in the terrible events of the war and they trust them. The communists muster millions of votes at the polls.(14)

On September 16 the Soviet Union representative introduced a lengthy resolution, which, since no Ukrainian proposal was submitted, can be regarded as the logical culmination of Manuilsky's efforts. In the first part of the resolution, Gromyko urged the Security Council to accept his version of the state of affairs in Greece and on its borders as fact (which essentially followed the views expressed by Manuilsky). The second part of his resolution contained four specific measures that the Council should use in its relations with the Greek government. In the first measure, the government of Greece was called upon to stop "the provocative activities of the aggressive monarchist elements on the Greko-Albanian frontier." The second measure advocated abandonment by Greek authorities of "the agitation regarding the state of war which is said to exist between Greece and Algania. . . ." In the third and fourth recommendations, Gromyko proposed that the Greek government should "terminate the persecution of national minorities in Greece" and that the problem be kept on the Council's agenda until the Greek government acceded to these measures.(15) At the next meeting, on September 17, the Ukrainian Foreign Minister asked the Security Council to adopt the USSR's resolution.(16)

The seventieth meeting of the Security Council, held on September 20, dealt for the last time with the Ukrainian complaint. Several resolutions were voted on, including one submitted by the United States.(17) The Soviet proposal was presented first and was rejected; the American proposal fared no better and failed also, despite eight affirmative votes. When several other resolutions were likewise voted down, the discussions came to an end.(18)

Manuilsky's diplomatic talents, supported by the Soviet Union, had not been sufficient to score a victory against the pro-Western government of Greece and the United Kingdom. The overwhelming majority of the Security Council voted against the Soviet resolution, which aimed at condemining and descrediting the policies of the only non-communist government left in the Balkan peninsula. Had the resolution passed, Great Britain, too, would have been humiliated in the eyes of the world.(19) It should be emphasized, however, that the representatives of the USSR and the Ukrainian SSR could hardly have harbored any illusions about the adoption of the Soviet proposal. Why, then, did they offer it?

In attempting to answer this question, one may argue that the fate of the proposal could not have been of paramount important to the Soviets. After all, it constituted only a small part of the debate on the confused situation in Greece; this situation, in Manuilsky's able hands, became the sounding board of communist propaganda. The Security Council, at the time the most respected organ of the UN, was turned into an arena for charges against the Greek government, threatened by destruction from its own communists. The Ukrainian complain was meant to show how unhealthy and bankrupt this government wab, and also attempted to evoke sympathy for the struggling Greek Communist Party, as well as for Albania. Manuilsky's rhetoric also hit Britain for giving military assistance to Athens; it was obvious that the Kremlin leadership wanted the British out of Greece, for their presence could have spelled the difference between success and failure of the communist-led rebellion. Had the rebellion succeeded, it would have brought the last non-communist Balkan country into the Soviet camp, opening Moscow's door to the eastern Mediterranean, while bypassing the Straits.(20)

Friend of Zionist Israel

The Ukrainian delegation also displayed considerable interest in UN debates on the Palestine question. After World War I Palestine had become a British mandate under the general supervision of the League of Nations. In the period between the First and the Second World Wars, the situation in this small Near East land was characterized by intense Jewish-Arab antagonism. Both peoples desired some sort of a state.The Arabs wanted an independent Palestine in which they, being a majority, hoped to rule; the Jews, however, inspired and led by the Zionists, thought in terms of a "National Home," which was another name for the Jewish state. The immigration of Jews to Palestine tended to strengthen the Zionist ideal and was bitterly opposed by the Arabs. After World War II the irreconcilable differences between the two sides became even more pronounced, and Great Britain, unable to solve the growing Arab-Jewish conflict, decided to submit the matter to the UN General Assembly. On November 29, 1947, the required two-thirds majority of the Assembly voted for the partition of Palestine into Arab and Jewish parts. On the whole, the Jews were satisfied, but the Arabs considered the Assembly resolution unacceptable. The British were soon to leave Palestine, and when, on May 14, 1948, their high commissioner departed, the Jews proclaimed the establishment of the state of Israel. Washington extended *de facto* recognition of the new state on the same day and Moscow extended *de jure* recognition three days later. Meanwhile, several Arab states sent their troops into Palestine to hlep the Palestinian Arabs in their struggle against the Jews. The Security Council met on May 15 to deal with the problem.(21)

On May 18, 1948, at the 294th meeting of the Security Council, Tarasenko spoke twice on the need for a speedy solution to the Palestine crisis. Expressing concern over the mounting casualties in the "armed struggle" which was "developing into a war between certain States of the Near East," he suggested that the Security Council should stop wasting time on unnecessary discussions and take appropriate measures to terminate hostilities.(22) Two days later, he voiced his disagreement with the representative of the United Kingdom over the latter's statement(23) that his government had doubts whether, from the legal point of view, there existed a danger to international peace resulting from the situation in Palestine. Tarasenko believed that the "legal premises of a vague and doubtful character" should be discarded in favor of facts which showed that several states had dispatched their armed forces into Palestine with "a definite military and political purpose." However, since the state of Israel was certain to fight in defense of the territory it claimed, it was obvious that this presented a threat to "peace and security in wide areas of the Near and Middle East." After arguing against the British interpretation of the events unfolding in Palestine, Tarasenko attempted to prove that the United Kingdom was partly responsible for the disorders taking place there. He drew the attention of the Council to the military activities of the Arab Legion directed against the state of Israel, stressing that these troops of the Kingdom of Transjordan were actually a part of Britain's armed forces.

> In these circumstances, how can the United Kingdom Government be an impartial judge or observer of this matter? Of course, it cannot. The United Kingdom Government must assume full responsibility, both moral and legal, for the actions of the Transjordan armed forces, for the fact that up to the present day it has been impossible to stop the fighting in Palestine. . . .

Tarasenko further stated that since the Arab Legion was fighting the Jews and since there was an alliance between Transjordan and the United Kingdom, it was quite logical "to conclude that the United Kingdom is both legally and *de facto* in a state of war with the State of Israel, and is a participant in the armed conflict." Charging Britain with a desire to dominate Palestine and to not allow the Jews and the Arabs to determine their own political fate, Tarasenko said that the Palestine problem would have been already solved for the benefit of these peoples, had it not been for the opposition of the United Kingdom.(24)

By this time the verbal assaults and reasoning of the Ukrainian delegation were becoming very familiar to the British. From the outset of Security Council activities, the London government was antagonized and attacked by the Ukrainian diplomats. Was there a pattern to this? Was there a real aim to discredit one of the two remaining great Western powers? In the atmosphere of growing tension between the two hostile camps, Soviet and Western, it could not have been otherwise. As will be seen later, much more was at stake than merely British reputation.

On May 27 the Ukrainian delegation noted with displeasure that hostilities still continued in Palestine, contrary to the resolution of the United States adopted by the Security Council on May 22, which called on all parties to end fighting.(25) On this occasion, Tarasenko, pointing out that a military struggle was in progress "as a result of the unlawful invasion by a number of States of the territory of Palestine," regretted that "certain circles" of several Arab countries were not defending the interests of their peoples, but rather those of the British empire. He urged taking more effective steps to ameliorate the existing situation — without, however, presenting a concrete proposal.(26) A proposal was made by Gromyko on the same day, suggesting that the Security Council should order both sides to stop "military operations within thirty-six hours after the adoption by the Security Council of this resolution".(27) A rather lengthy resolution was also submitted at the same meeting by the British representative.(28)

On the following day, Britain's proposal was harshly criticized by Tarasenko, who described it as being one-sided and anti-Jewish. "It is no exaggeration to say," commented Tarasenko, "that the United Kingdom resolution is designed to stifle the State of Israel and the Jewish people in Palestine." The resolution was calculated to strengthen Arab forces which had invaded Palestine and also to weaken Israel; its adoption would mean that, "besides being subjected to invasion by the armies of seven States," the Jewish people would "also be subjected to moral, material, economic, and perhaps other sanctions of the United Nations." Such a biased proposal as Britain's could not be accepted, he declared. He then asked for the adoption of the Soviet resolution, which he thought would satisfy both Jews and Arabs in Palestine.(29) Despite the fact that this resolution was supported by several countries including the United States and France, it was not carried.(30) The maligned British proposal, on the other hand, received most of the votes after some minor changes were made.(31)

Both parties to the conflict agreed to the cease-fire, and on June 10 the four-week truce came into effect. Since it was to expire on July 9, the UN mediator for Palestine, Count Folke Bernadotte, asked the United Nations to try to prevent the resumption of hostilities by calling upon the opposing sides to prolong the truce.(32)

On July 7, at the start of the meeting, an interesting development occurred. Manuilsky, in his capacity as the Security Council president, invited several representatives of the parties involved in the Palestine conflict — as was commonly practiced in such matters — to take seats at the Council table. One of those invited was Aubrey (Abba) Eban, spokesman for the Palestine Jews. Before this meeting, Eban had officially represented the Jewish Agency for Palestine; now he was addressed by the president of the Council as the representative of the state of Israel. Since most of the countries whose delegations sat in the Council did not recognize the Israeli state, the president's procedure was immediately challenged by Ambassador Cadogan on behalf of the United Kingdom, and also by other delegates. Tsiang of China noted that "in changing the title of the representative of the Jewish Agency, the President acted without authorization of the Council." Gromyko remained silent, and only one delegate spoke in favor of the president's action: Philip C. Jessup of the United States, whose government had also recognized Israel. Outnumbered, Manuilsky fought back, but his defeat was imminent. The spokesman for Egypt, invited to the Security Council as one of the parties to the conflict, said that the president's move was "against the position of eight out of the eleven members represented in the Security Counil." Finally, the communist diplomat decided to solve the problem by voting and asked who was in favor of his ruling. Since it was obvious that the majority would not vote for such a ruling, it was difficult to understand Manuilsky's move, but the situation became clearer when Gromyko stated "that the correct way to proceed would be exactly the reverse. We should vote on the question who is against the President's ruling?" Only five delegates voted against it. The ruling was sustained, and henceforth Eban represented not merely an agency, but a sovereign state. It was a masterful performance by the Soviet diplomats.(33)

After this brief but significant exchange, Manuilsky, speaking as the representative of Ukrainian SSR, expressed his objections to Count Bernadotte's activities in Palestine(34) and accused the mediator of working contrary to the General Assembly resolution of November 29, 1974, which

> provided for the creation of two independent States in Palestine — a Jewish and an Arab State — and the formation of an economic union between them. Mr. Bernadotte annulled this decision and suggested to the Jews and the Arabs that they should in fact create one State on a federal basis and hand over foreign policy and military defense to a central government camouflaged as a Council of the Union.

Again, in the case of Jerusalem, Manuilsky charged that the mediator had a solution different than the General Assembly's. Whereas the Assembly's resolution was to internationalize the city, Manuilsky accused Bernadotte of promising it to the Arabs. Bernadotte's proposal to make Transjordan a part of the Palestine Union also came under attack.

Manuilsky charged that the apparent reason for this plan was to make King Abdullah of Transjordan "the head of the dual Jewish-Arab State." Such a development, he said, would be quite disastrous for Israel, since Abdullah, besides being "a persecutor of the Jewish population," desired "the complete destruction of the Jewish State in Palestine." Bernadotte's plan to have Palestine under Abdullah was not only dangerous to the Jews, but to the Arabs as well, and was designed to serve the interests of the United Kingdom and possibly other states. Manuilsky told the Security Council that his delegation would abstain from voting on the resolution to prolong the truce;(35) it would do so not because it opposed the truce in principle, but because Bernadotte's proposals should be rejected as being in violation of the UN General Assembly resolution. Bernadotte should be advised by the Security Council, he asserted, "not to exceed the powers granted him, but to abide by the decisions of the General Assembly."(36) When the British truce proposal was put to a vote, it was adopted with only three abstentions, including those of Ukraine and the Soviet Union.(37)

The accepted proposal proved to be quite meaningless; soon after it was adopted, hostilities were resumed in Palestine. On July 15, Manuilsky, speaking again as representative of Soviet Ukraine, and not as president of the Council, once more attacked the mediator's role in the Arab-Jewish dispute. Repeating that Bernadotte had deviated from the Assembly decision of November 29, 1947, he said, in reference to the mediator's proposal, that

> neither the State of Israel nor the Arab States have accepted this plan which only obscured the clear question of creating two States — an Arab State and a Jewish State — in Palestine. The plan still further inflamed nationalistic passions and hastened the collapse of the truce.

The Ukrainian foreign minister also criticized Count Bernadotte's suggestion, made on July 13,(38) with regard to the plebiscite in Palestine.

> The Mediator began by suggesting a plebiscite for Jerusalem only; but then, in a surge of creative improvisation, he proposed extending it to the whole of Palestine. . . . He cannot but be aware that the adoption of such a proposal would mean the liquidation of the State of Israel, to which, naturally, the Government of Israel would not agree.

As expected, Manuilsky chided Great Britain for its behavior in the Near East conflict; apparently the Soviet diplomat was trying to impress on the Arabs the danger of British domination in the area. Pointing out that British withdrawal from Palestine did not mean the end of Britain's colonial designs in the Near East, and drawing attention to the alleged methods they used to divide the Jews and the Arabs from the other Arabs, he presented his interpretation of the Palestine strife. According to this view, the fight against Israel was a device by which Great Britain sought to divert the attention of the Arab world from its own troubles: a divice meant to paralyze the Arab "struggle for political and economic independence and for national revival." Manuilsky said he regretted that some Arabs had accused "the Soviet delegations of supporting one side of the Arab-Jewish dispute." Offering no denial, however, he said that "the Soviet people are people of principle; they always stand for what is right." To prove this, Manuilsky mentioned previous support given by the USSR delegation to Syria, Lebanon, and other Arab countires when these states wanted to rid themselves of foreign troops from their land.

Continuing his assertions about the policy of principle, which, he said, was pursued by the Soviet delegations in general, and in the Palestinian case in particular, he criticized United States Palestinian policy for its "ambiguities, contradictions and hesitations." The U.S. position was explained by two influences on U.S. policy makers. One, supporting the establishment of the Israeli state, derived its strength from the Jewish population living in the United States, which exerted a certain influence on American "political circles." The second influence was U.S. oil companies, which were "trying to secure concessions to exploit the oil resources to be found in the Arab States." This latter influence stood against the Assembly resolution of November 29, and its ascendency "wouldnot portend any good for the State of Israel."

The Arab countries, too, continued Manuilsky, would be at a disadvantage "if two oil groups of different national origin came to an agreement behind their backs on the division of spheres of interest in the Near East," and an agreement of this nature would hardly help to enhance "the national sovereignty of the Arab States." On the whole, there existed a danger that certain powers, (e.g., the United Kingdom, the United States, and France) might reach some sort of understanding among themselves which would profit neither the Arabs nor the Jews.(39)

At the same meeting the Security Council adopted the amended United States proposal that ordered the hostile sides to stop fighting. Both Jews and Arabs accepted the truce, and by July 18 it went into effect, although sporadic clashes continued.(40) In mid-October 1948, however, serious fighting broke out between Israeli and Egyptian forces in the Negev area. Ralph Bunche, acting UN mediator for

Palestine,(41) appealed to both parties to terminate the hostilities. In reply, the governments of Egypt and Israel stated that they had given orders for a cease-fire. On October 28 the acting mediator told the Security Council of his attempts to bring about a withdrawal of the Egyptian and Israeli troops to positions they occupied on October 14 — that is, before the start of the hostilities. The Council then took upon itself the task of helping solve the newest crisis in the Negev sector.(42)

On that same day, October 14, the United Kingdom and China had submitted a joint draft resolution(43) which they reintroduced the next day in a revised form.(44) Since this revised resolution was in need of additional revision, the Canadian delegate proposed the establishment of a subcommittee to deal with this matter, suggesting that Ukraine be one of its members.(45) Manuilsky remarked that his delegation was opposed to the joint British-Chinese proposal, but "if the President of the Security Council and the Council itself consider that all viewpoints should be represented on the subcommittee, then the Ukrainian delegation will sit on that sub-committee and co-operate with it."(46)

On November 4, two resolutions were presented to the Security Council, one by the majority of the subcommittee, the other by the representative of the Ukrainian SSR. The Ukrainian draft resolution read:

> The *Security Council*
> *Taking into consideration* the conditions set out in the resolution of 19 October, which could be carefully examined as a basis for further negotiations between the two parties,
> *Calls* upon the two parties to begin negotiations, either directly or through the intermediary of a United Nations representative, on the basis of the aforementioned resolution, with a view to the peaceful settlement of unresolved questions, and
> *Instructs* the Acting Mediator to offer his good offices to the parties for this purpose and to assist in the conduct of such negotiations.

After submitting the resolution, Tarasenko observed that the merit of the proposal lay in the fact that it constituted a development of the October 19 resolution and that it would eliminate the contradiction between the two resolutions of November 4. He said that it also stressed "the idea reflected in the resolution of 19 October on negotiations between parties" and expressed the hope that the Council would adopt the Ukrainian proposal.(47)

Compared with Ukraine's resolution, the subcommittee's resolution was a rather lengthy document. Among other things, it called upon the governments of Egypt and Israel "to withdraw those of their forces which had advanced beyond the positions held on 14 October, the Acting Mediator being authorized to establish provisional lines beyond which no movement of troops shall take place."(48) The sesential difference between the two proposals manifested itsvlf by omission, in the Ukrainian resolution, of referral to withdrawal of opposing forces to positions held on October 14.(49)

Abba Eban favored the Ukrainian resolution.(50) He maintained that the Negev area was an integral part of the Jewish state "to which the authority and the duty of the Government of Israel must rightfully extend and continue to extend," and he regarded the presence of the Egyptian army in the Negev as an invasion. Further, he accused the United Kingdom, "which first sponsored a resolution requesting the withdrawl of Israeli forces from their positions," of trying "to detach the greater part of Israel, without Israel's consent, from its frontiers." The representative of Egypt, on the other hand, although not fully satisfied with the subcommittee's proposal, preferred it to the Ukrainian proposal.(51) Finally, when the resolutions were put to a vote, the subcommittee's proposal, as amended on the initiative of the United States delegation, was adopted. The proposal advanced by Ukraine was supported only by the two Soviet delegations.(52)

In the Security Council debates on Palestine, the Ukrainian SSR, together with the Soviet Union, consistently supported the Zionist cause. Such an attitude obviously pleased the Jews and antagonized the Arabs, both in Palestine and in the Arab states. Why did the Ukrainian delegation follow this course? What were the motives behind the actions of Manuilsky and Tarasenko?

It seems that, as in the Indonesian and Greek debates, Soviet intentions in the Palestinian matter were to hasten the departure of the dominant European power from the area in question: the Dutch had to leave Indonesia and the British Greece. This diminution of the strength of the Western camp meant a potential increase in the strength of the Soviet bloc. Yet, while Greece lay within the reach of Bolshevik strategic power and was of immediate concern to Moscow, the same was not true of Palestine. No communist-inspired civil war was raging within its borders, and Moscow could have no immediate hope of penetrating that region.

It was logical, then, to criticize the British for their Palestinian policies, thus contributing to British desire to abandon the controversial and burdensome mandate. But why did Ukraine cultivate Arab displeasure by siding with the Jews? To be sure, the Ukrainian representatives showed a restraint in their statements toward Arab actions; they conserved their verbal blasts for use against the United Kingdom and attempted to impress upon the Arab peoples the undesirable qualities of British imperialism — but a pro-Jewish tendency was hardly a mirage. Such a tendency, which must have been a policy decision at the time, appears to have been based on the belief that the Arab "ruling circles" generally followed British leadership in Middle East politics, the factor Moscow wished to eliminate. The Zionists who had fought to establish the Jewish state in Palestine, however, were in no mood to pursue pro-British policies, especially when these stood in the way of Isreali independence. Since there was obvious estrangement or even hostility between the Israelis and Great Britain, the Soviets had a reason to support "one side in the Arab-Jewish dispute," finding in it at least a temporary ally.(53) Then, again, the mere existence of the Israeli state in the Near East upset the regional equilibrium that could erupt into a hostile confrontation to be used by an expansionist power for its own purposes. This could not have been overlooked by the Kremlin rulers, a factor which gave them another reason for defending and aiding the Jewish side.

Footnotes

(1) Churchill, Vol. VI, *Triumph and Tragedy,* 227. This "deal" was proposed by the British prime minister.

(2) See footnote 20 of this chapter.

(3) See D. George Kousoulas, *Revolution and Defeat: The Story of the Greek Communist Party* (London: Oxford University Press, 1965); Edgar O'Ballance, *The Greek Civil War, 1944-1949* (New York: Praeger, 1966); Churchill, Vol. VI, *Triumph and Tragedy;* Stephen G. Xydis, *Greece and the Great Powers, 1944-1947: Prelude to the Truman Doctrine* (Thessaloniki: Institute for Balkan Studies, 1963). The author discusses the Ukrainian complaint in some details on pp. 335-346 and 349-355.

(4) Security Council, *Records,* First Year, Supplement No. 5. The Ukrainian foreign minister denounced Greece "as a troublemaker and potential threat to peace" at the Paris Peace Conference on August 22 (see *The New York Times,* August 23, 1946), p. 1. At this conference the Greek government demanded the cession of Northern Epirus (Southern Albania).

(5) Security Council, *Records,* First Year, No. 4, 54th meeting, August 28, 1946, 33-38.

(6) *Ibid.,* No. 7, 59th meeting, September 3, 1946, 173-197. China, Egypt, France, Mexico, Poland, and the USSR, and the U.S. voted in favor; the United Kingdom and the Netherlands voted against; Australia and Brazil abstained.

(7) This newspaper was published in New York by Ralph McAllister from 1940 to 1948.

(8) Article 2 (7) of the Charter reads, in part, "Nothing contained in the present Charter shall authorize the United Nations to intervene in matters which are essentially within the domestic jurisdiction of any state. . . ."

(9) *Ibid.*, No. 8, 60th meeting, September 4, 1946, 201-212. The text of Manuilsky's speech in Ukrainian appeared in *Radians'ka Ukraina,* September 6, 1946.

(10) For a perceptive view on this problem, see James Reston's short article, "Expediency of Admitting Ukraine into U.N. Arises" (*The New York Times,* September 5, 1946), p. 2.

(11) Security Council, *Records,* First Year, No. 9, 61st and 62nd meetings, September 5, 1946, 214-240. By "proper quarters," Dendramis meant, of course, Moscow.

(12) *Ibid.*, No. 9, 62nd meeting, September 5, 1946, 241-249.

(13) *Ibid.*, No. 10, 64th meeting, September 9, 1946, 267-271.

(14) *Ibid.*, No. 11, 65th meeting, September 13, 1946, 184-194. The text in Ukrainian appeared in *Radians'ka Ukraina,* September 13, 1946.

(15) Security Council, *Records,* First Year, No. 13, 67th meeting, September 16, 1946, 334-335.

(16) *Ibid.*, No. 14, 68th meeting, September 17, 1946, 353-359.

(17) This resolution suggested the establishment of a commission composed of three persons, which would look into the Balkan situation (*ibid.*, No. 16, 70th meeting, September 20, 1946, 396).

(18) *Ibid.*, 406-422. Only the USSR and Poland voted in favor of the Soviet proposal.

(19) Actually, the Soviet resolution contained no strong words against the United Kingdom. It merely said that the Greek monarchists were "exploiting the presence of the British troops," and that "in spite of the repeated declarations by the Minister for Foreign Affairs of Great Britain that these troops would be withdrawn after the elections of 31 March 1946," they remained in Greece. The language was restrained but the meaning was clear: British troops should leave Greek territory as soon as possible. Security Council, *Records,* First Year, No. 13, 67th meeting, September 16, 1946, 334.

(20) Major O'Ballance believed that Stalin definitely had a hand in the decision of the Greek Communist Party to renew the civil war. He wrote that "Stalin, approving the formation of the Democratic Army (the successor to the defunct ELAS), asked Yugoslavia and Albania to give clandestine material aid and support. He also vaguely promised to help, but no supplies or arms ever arrived from the Soviet Union" (see O'Ballance, 122).

Discussing Moscow's postwar pressure on both Greece and Turkey, Prof. Adam Ulam pointed out that "in their attempt to gain a foothold in the eastern Mediterranean, the Soviets continued what has been one of the oldest traditions of Russian foreign policy. . . . During the war Stalin tacitly accepted Churchill's insistence that Greece should remain within the British sphere and, in view of the British statesman's obduracy, dropped his demand for bases in Turkey. But the Soviets could not have been unmindful that the British anti-Communist intervention in Greece in 1944 received a bad press in the United States and among some Labour Party circles in Britain." Ulam further observed that since at that time Washington did not fully support the British in their "efforts to keep those countries out of the Soviet sphere," it was reasonable to assume for the Kremlin that, after Churchill's defeat in the election, the Soviets could crown their endeavors with success there. After all, "Greece was now surrounded by Communist-dominated states, and in the summer of 1946 the Communist guerrilla movement renewed its operations there on a large scale. It could count on bases and sanctuaries in Yugoslavia, Albania and Bulgaria. The usually disorderly state of Greek politics enhanced the danger that the little country would share the fate of her neighbors'' (Adam B. Ulam, *Expansion and Coexistence; The History of Soviet Foreign Policy, 1917-1967* (New York: Praeger, 1968), pp. 429-430.

Later however, when the United States had intervened in Greece to save the country from communist takeover (Truman Doctrine, March 1947), the Soviet prospects of having a new member in the Moscow orbit had drastically diminished. In fact,by early 1948 Stalin was quite pessimistic about the outcome of the Greek communist uprising. As reported by Djilas, who was present at a Kremlin meeting of Soviet, Yugoslav, and Bulgarian representatives on February 10, the Bolshevik leader insisted that the Greek communists had no chance of success. ''What do you think'' he declared, ''that Great Britain and the United States — the United States, the most powerful state in the world — will permit you to break their line of communication in the Mediterranean Sea! Nonsense. And we have no navy. The uprising in Greece must be stopped, and as quickly as possible'' (Milovan Djilas, *Conversations with Stalin* (New York: Harcourt, Brace and World, 1962), p. 182).

(21) See A. M. Hyamson, *Palestine under the Mandate, 1920-1948* (London: Methuen, 1951); L. F. R. Williams, *The State of Israel* (New York: Macmillan, 1957).

(22) Security Council, *Records,* Third Year, No. 68, 294th meeting, May 18, 1948, 2-3, 13-14.

(23) Made at the previous meeting (see *ibid.,* No. 69, 296th meeting, May 18, 1948, 3-4.

(24) *Ibid.,* No. 70, 297th meeting, May 20, 1948, 4-7.

(25) See *ibid.,* No. 72, 302nd meeting, May 22, 1948, 37-66.

(26) *Ibid.,* No. 75, 306th meeting, May 27, 1948, 7-9.

(27) *Ibid.,* 17-18. It also stated that ''the situation in Palestine constitutes a threat to peace and security within the meaning of Article 39 of the Charter . . .'' (Reference to Chapter VII, Article 39; this chapter is entitled ''Action with Respect to Threats to the Peace, Breaches of the Peace, and Acts of Aggression''). The resolution was similar to the one proposed by the United States on May 17 and adopted, with important amendments, on May 22.

(28) *Ibid.,* 29-30. This proposal called upon the participants in the conflict to stop military activities for four weeks, and to promise not to ''introduce fighting personnel or men of military age into Palestine during the cease-fire''; it also appealed to the opposing sides and ''all Governments to refrain from importing war material into Palestine during the cease-fire'' and asked ''all concerned'' to assist the UN mediator in his task, stating that rejection of this resolution might bring ''action under Chapter VII of the UN Charter.''

(29) *Ibid.,* No. 76, 307th meeting, May 28, 1948, 13-17.

(30) *Ibid.,* No. 77, 310 meeting, May 29, 1948, 35-37. Before the vote was taken, the USSR delegation amended its own proposal, accusing the Arab states of noncompliance with the May 22 resolution.

(31) *Ibid.,* 38-63.

(32) See *Yearbook* 1947-1948, 433.

(33) Security Council, *Records,* Third Year, No. 93, 330th meeting, July 7, 1948. Also see *The New York Times,* July 8, p. 3 and 9, p. 2, 1948.

(34) He had in mind particularly the mediator's suggestions concerning the

Palestine problem, addressed to both the Arabs and the Jews and rejected by both sides. See *Yearbook,* 1947-1948, 432.

(35) Heeding the mediator's appeal, this resolution, submitted by the United Kingdom, said that "*The Security Council, taking into consideration* the telegram from the United Nations Mediator dated 5 July 1948, *addresses* an urgent appeal to the interested parties to accept in principle the prolongation of the truce for such a period as may be decided upon in consultation with the Mediator" (Security Council, *Records,* Third Year, No. 93, 331st meeting, July 7, 1948, 35).

(36) *Ibid.,* 27-32.

(37) *Ibid.,* 35.

(38) *Ibid.,* No. 95, 333rd meeting, July 13, 1948, 8-10.

(39) *Ibid.,* No. 97, 338th meeting, July 15, 1948, 25-30.

(40) See *Yearbook,* 1947-1948, 441-443.

(41) Count Folke Bernadotte had been assassinated on September 17, 1948, in Jerusalem.

(42) See *Yearbook,* 1948-1949, 177-179.

(43) Security Council, *Records,* Third Year, No. 122, 374th meeting, October 28, 1948, 12-13.

(44) *Ibid.,* No. 123, 375th meeting, October 29, 1948, 2-3.

(45) *Ibid.,* 19-20. The resolution read, "*The Security Council resolves* that a sub-committee be established consisting of the representatives of the United Kingdom, China, France, Belgium and the Ukrainian Soviet Socialist Republic to consider all the amendments and revisions which have been or may be suggested to the second revised draft resolution" (*ibid.,* 22).

(46) *Ibid.,* 21.

(47) *Ibid.,* No. 124, 376th meeting, November 4, 1948, 6. The October 19 resolution dealt with the troublesome Negev situation and saw its amelioration in "an immediate and effective cease-fire." It also concerned itslef, among other things, with the possible "withdrawal of both parties from any positions not occupied at the time of the outbreak" and the possible negotiations between the two parties in the Negev dispute, with or without United Nations intermediaries (*ibid.,* No. 118, 367th meeting, October 19, 1948, 37-38).

(48) *Yearbook,* 1948-1949, 180-181.

(49) It was common knowledge that the Israelis were winning in the Negev and trying to consolidate their territorial gains. In these circumstances, to go back to the October 14 line was unthinkable for them.

(50) Security Council, *Records,* Third Year, No. 124, 376th meeting, November 4, 1948, 10-20.

(51) *Ibid.,* 20-22.

(52) *Ibid.,* 377th meeting, November 4, 1948, 38-46.

(53) Several years later, as the Suez crisis in 1956 clearly demonstrated, the UN delegations of Ukraine and the Soviet Union took an opposite position in the long-standing dispute. This remarkable reversal of policy can be explained by the fact that, by 1956 or even sooner, the Israelis showed a marked preference for the Western bloc, while some Arabs, particularly the Egyptians, after internal changes in their countries, were displaying anti-British and anti-Western sentiments. This then opened real possibilities for Soviet-Arab cooperation.

CHAPTER 6
DEALING WITH COMMUNISM — TRUE AND HERETICAL
Defender of Communist Czechoslovakia

On March 10, 1948, the representative of Czechoslovakia to the UN, Jan Papanek, delivered a note to the Secretary-General Trygve Lie of the United Nations in which he said that his country's government "had been undermined and openly placed in jeopardy on February 22, 1948, through force by a Communist minority." Papanek further stated that "this Communist minority was encouraged and given promise of help if necessary, by the representatives of the Government of the Union of Soviet Socialist Republics . . ." and that the actions of the USSR constituted a violation of Article 2, Paragraph 4, of the UN Charter.(1) Since, in Papanek's view, such a development, besides "suppressing the freedom and independence of Czechoslovakia," was "likely to endanger the maintenance of international peace and security," he called upon the Security Council to investigate the situation under Article 34 of the Charter.(2) This request, however, was not accepted by Secretary-General Lie on the grounds that it could not be regarded as coming from the representative of a UN member state, but from an individual person.(3) On March 12 the Chilean representative submitted a letter to the secretary-general, drawing attention to Papanek's communication and requesting that the Czechoslovak case be brought before the Security Council.(4) The Chilean complaint against the Soviet Union concerning the situation in Czechoslovakia signaled the beginning of an acrimonious debate in which the Ukrainian delegation played a prominent role.

The debate opened on March 17 at the 268th meeting of the Security Council, with a strenuous effort on the part of Gromyko and Tarasenko to bar the Chilean letter from the agenda. The Ukrainian representative argued that "no one with a genuine regard for the authority of the United Nations can possibly allow the slanderous Chilean document" to be considered by the Council, for to do that "would mean a direct and completely unjustified intervention by the Security Council in the internal affairs of the Czechoslovak Republic. . . ." Like Gromyko before him, Tarasenko reminded the members of the Council of Article 2, Paragraph 7, which, briefly stated, does not allow the United Nations to interfere in the domestic affairs of states. Additionally, "the inclusion on the Security Council's agenda of the Chilean letter, with its calumnies about the Soviet Union, would constitute an insult to the 200 million men and women of the Soviet Union.''(5) When the vote was taken on whether to add the Chilean complaint to the agenda, the vote was nine to two, in favor of the inclusion.(6)

The next step was the seating of the Chilean delegate at the Council's table in order that he might make an additional statement. Gromyko said nothing about this; Tarasenko vehemently objected. ''What concern,'' asked the Ukrainian delegate, ''even the remotest, has Chile with past and present events in Czechoslovakia, which the Security Council is now being asked to discuss?'' After all, he proclaimed, the Chilean letter contained nothing ''apart from a lying story told by a Czechoslovak renegade.''(7) Nevertheless, the majority voted to invite the Chilean delegate, Santa Cruz, to participate in the discussion, and he subsequently made a lengthy statement accusing the Czech communist minority and the government of the Soviet Union of effecting a *coup d'etat* in Czechoslovakia. As a result, the Chilean diplomat continued, Czechoslovakia was deprived of its independence and became ''an unconditional instrument of the Soviet Union's expansionist policy of European domination.'' Quoting from Jan Papanek's letter and questioning the ''empty formalism'' of the United Nations, which did not allow the Czechoslovak diplomat to state his case, Santa Cruz asked the Security Council to hear Papanek.(8)

In the 1946 debates on Indonesia and Greece that were initiated by the representative of the Ukrainian SSR, the charges were made by the communist side, and the accused found themselves in a rather unenviable position. However, no Indonesian or Greek representative or ex-representative appeared to bolster Manuilsky's arguments. No Indonesian or Greek representative had voiced a protest in the UN, for obviously the situation in Czechoslovakia was of a different kind. Papanek, a permanent representative of his government in the UN, spoke against that government after, as he stated, it had been taken over by the Czechoslovak communists with the help of the USSR. It was he who became the chief accuser of the Soviet government, while Chile's role in the matter remained clearly of a secondary importance. Because of this, the Czechoslovak question appeared to be built on a firmer foundation than were the Indonesian and the Greek matters, raised solely by an outsider — Soviet Ukraine.

In 1946, when the Ukrainian SSR demanded to sit at the Council table to present additional information on the matter under consideration, Manuilsky would have been quite indignant had he been barred from this role. Now with great zeal, Tarasenko was opposing any participation by the Chilean representative in the debate; he even fought against including the complaint on the agenda. Tarasenko maintained that Chile was not competent to discuss Czechoslovak affairs — but was Ukrain'es competence any greater in the case of Indonesia? Manuilsky had once said that the Soviet people pursued a policy of principle. If so, there must have been a dviation from this policy at the very start of the Czechoslovak debate.

In spite of protests by Tarasenko and Gromyko, on March 22 the Council decided to invite Papanek to take part in the discussion. In his statement Papanek pointed out that the communist coup in his country was inevitable; because of the coming general elections in May the communists were bound to be disappointed, and, therefore, had to look for a drastic solution of their difficulties. Papanek said that

> the coup had to take place, because it was clear that the Communist Party not only would not gain in the elections, but would suffer a loss which would result in Communist decline in other countries of Central and Eastern Europe. Neither the Communist Party nor the USSR could permit such a political development at this time. Could someone perhaps suggest that the USSR was not interested in the outcome of the elections, or would someone perhaps claim that the coup was necessary if the Czechoslovak nation wished to return a Communist majority in free and secret elections?

He further stated that the coup, although carried out by Czechoslovak leaders such as Klement Gottwald, Zdenek Fierlinger, and others, could not be regarded "as a purely internal matter," but there was evidence of Soviet "indirect aggression," "political infiltration," and even "direct intervention" in the affairs of his country. Citing several examples as proof of these charges, Papanek told the Council that the Czechoslovak situation constituted "a threat to international peace and security referred to in Article 34 of the Charter"; and he warned Council members that "the aggressor, sure of his strength, after allowing time for consolidating his newly acquired position, cannot long refrain from taking another step forward on the path of aggression." The former representative of Prague to the United Nations made his concluding remarks by appealing to the UN to not "fail the freedom-loving people of Czechoslovakia, who are now terrrorized, silenced and enslaved."(9)

At that same meeting, Tarasenko questioned the truth of the charges made by Chile and Papanek, presented another version of the February events in Czechoslovakia, and drew the Security Council's attention to various developments all over the world, apparently connected with the case. Tarasenko said that the Chilean letter — "this extraordinarily dirty and calumnious document" — in spite of objections to the contrary, finally got a hearing and now the Ukrainian delegation was obliged to discuss the matter. However, in dealing with the problem, he would dwell neither on the role of Chile nor on Papanek's "childish slander," but would be "chiefly interested in other facts and those other forces which have compelled this question to be raised before the Security Council." Quoting a particular article that appeared in the Czechoslovak press, Tarasenko tried to prove the existence of a reactionary conspiracy in Czechoslovakia — even prior to the alleged communist coup — whose purpose was to establish an anti-communist regime. The conspiracy, insisted Tarasenko, was linked to Washington and London, and such well-known persons as Winston Churchill and former ambassador William C. Bullitt were connected with it. Tarasenko argued that:

> At the last moment, however, the plans of the domestic and foreign conspirators were upset. It is no secret that the Communist Party of Czechoslovakia played a decisive and leading role in the wrecking of these plans. That was bound to arouse storms of anger and to call forth torrents of slander against the Party from all those who were backing and organizing the Czechoslovak conspirators and had placed their hopes in them.

It was wrong to "accuse the USSR of interference in the internal affairs of Czechoslovakia" because it had "nothing to do with this matter." The Soviet troops had long ago left Czechoslovakia and its people were free to determine their own fate. Tarasenko had no doubt "that it is precisely in the Communist Party, and in those democratic elements which stand for democratic ideas in the economic and political life of their country, that the Czechoslovak people have placed their confidence." It was indeed hard to believe, he declared, that the Party which headed the government, held the power, and wielded a tremendous influence throughout the country would "organize a coup against itself."(10)

The Soviet Ukrainian delegation was evidently not satisfied with the defense of the Czechoslovak communists and the USSR, for Tarasenko then proceeded to criticize American — and, occasionally, British — behavior in the world, yet never losing sight of the central problem. From a basically defensive posture, his speech assumed an aggressive quality. Comparing the policies of the two antagonistic Great Powers, stated:

> The fiction of alleged USSR intervention in the internal affairs of Czechoslovakia was invented in order to direct world public opinion along a false path. There is in fact no evidence testifying to intervention by the USSR in the internal affairs of Czechoslovakia;

> but there are more than enough facts demonstrating the direct intervention of the United States in the internal affairs in many countries of the world — and intervention of a particularly flagrant and outrageous character.

Tarasenko wondered whether the whole story of the alleged communist coup in Czechoslovakia — a "Chilean fabrication" — was not devised as a means of concealing the policy of intervention and expansion practiced by Washington.(11)

The Ukrainian delegate delivered another speech on March 31. Largely ignoring the statement of the Chilean delegate made at the same meeting,(12) he concentrated his attack on the remarks of the British and French representatives.(13) Tarasenko noted that the speeches of these delegates contained not a single proof in support of the accusations raised by the Chilean letter and the former representative of Czechoslovakia; in spite of this, the spokesmen for these countries "have found it possible to make a series of crude and hostile attacks on the USSR and Czechoslovakia." Particularly displeased by Ambassador Cadogan's comparison of the political fate of Czechoslovakia with that of other East European countries,(14) he said:

> I do not know which is more evident in the speeches of the representatives of the United Kingdom and France: hostility towards the peoples living in the countries of the new democracy and the USSR, or ignorance and lack of desire to know what is really taking place in those countries.

The reference of the French delegate, Alexandre Parodi, to the events in Czechoslovakia which, he said, were deeply felt by his people because of the "old friendship" between the French and the Czechs, also did not go unnoticed by the Ukrainian diplomat, who asked "whether it was in the name of the French Government's friendship . . . that the French ruling circles . . . betrayed and sold out the people of Czechoslovakia to Hitler at Munich."(15)

It must have been clear to the members of the Security Council, including the French representative, Parodi, that this and similar statements served as a maneuver to divert the discussion from the subject under consideration. In rebuttal, the Frenchman not only explained why Paris did not go to war in 1938, but also asked Tarasenko what the Soviet Union did at that time to save Czechoslovakia, charging Moscow, in turn, with the partition of Poland.(16)

On April 29 Tarasenko continued the historical polemic directed against France, in which, Britain, too, received a share of the blame. Before he began, however, Tarasenko took issue with the United States delegate, who, according to Tarasenko, made "a series of unfounded and, in some cases, fantastic 'charges' . . . in regard to the Soviet Union."(17) In the course of his rebuttal of the American attitude toward the Czechoslovak case, he challenged U.S. Senator Warren Austin's preoccupation with the charge — also advanced by others — that the Soviet Union had violated the independence of Czechoslovakia by a threat of force. Pointing out that the U.S. representative could not produce any evidence of this, Tarasenko chided Washington, by stating that

> perhaps the actions of the Soviet Union which could be interpreted as a threat of use of force were similar to the recent visit of the United States warships, with a very definite purpose, in the waters surrounding Italy. Perhaps the threat of use of force on the part of the Soviet Union consisted in the fact that it was establishing hundreds of military, naval and air bases thousands of miles away from its own frontiers, as the United States of America is doing.

Turning his attention to the question raised by the French representative regarding Soviet efforts to aid Czechoslovakia against Hitler, Tarasenko attempted to show that the Soviet Union had been ready to defend the threatened country, had the French — as the Czech-Soviet treaty stipulated — decided to come to Czechoslovakia's assistance. Criticizing Paris (and London) for aquiescing in that country's seizure by Germany, he called the present French concern with the events of Czechoslovakia a "sheer mockery."(18)

As soon as he finished, he was again challenged by Parodi,(19) and the ensuing historical debate, which had but a slight connection with the Chilean complaint, could have been mistaken by uninformed visitors as a meeting of a historical society. In vain did the Argentinian representative try to suggest that "these historical reminiscences," although by themselves of great interest, "should not make us forget that we have business on hand." His call to "Let us finally try to finish with this question of Czechoslovakia!"(20) was disregarded by Gromyko, who, pursuing the reasoning of his Ukrainian colleague, advised the French and British representatives, among other things, to read Churchill's memoirs which would show that Czechoslovakia was betrayed by both France and the United Kingdom.(21) Cadogan replied that he had read them, but did not think that Churchill had "yet reached August 1939," obviously referring to the Nazi-Soviet Non-Aggression Pact. However, "even if all that has been said here about the historical past were true," the British delegate remarked, "what has that to do with the case under examination?" Finally, the president of the Security Council declared that since its members "have had ample opportunity to present their historical and other views,'' he would call for a vote on the resolution.(22)

In brief, the Chilean resolution suggested the creation of a subcommittee, composed of three members,(23) for the purpose of gathering additional evidence on the Czechoslovak situation and presenting it to the Security Council as soon as possible. It was decided to regard this proposal as one of substance, thus making possible the casting of the veto. Of course, the negative vote of the Soviet Union resulted in rejection of the proposal,(24) essentially ending the debate on Czechoslovakia.

The Czechoslovak dispute, in comparison with the ones previously discussed, was undoubtedly the most uncomfortable for the Soviets. While in the three previous debates no Soviet interests were threatened, here the accusers became the accused. The occasion, in terms of East-West confrontation, was fraught with political embarrassment for Moscow. Caught by Papanek's sudden revelation and Chile's complaint, the two Soviet delegations fought stubbornly to prevent the question from appearing on the agenda. When this delaying action proved to be abortive, they dealt with the matter directly. Concentrating only on the statements of the Ukrainian representative, one must admit that Tarasenko's was a brilliant performance. Starting from what appeared to be an entirely defensive position, he launched his verbal assaults, applying the pressure until the very end. The Council was told that, instead of a communist conspiracy and coup, there was really an attempt on the part of reactionaries, with the connivance of the United States and the United Kingdom, to seize power in Czechoslovakia. Thus, the very weapons of the accusers were turned against them, and, as if that were not enough, the Western camp, especially the U.S., was subjected to heavy bombardment for a multitude of sins, both present and past. History is but an instrument of politics, according to one view, and it served its purpose in the Council. A careful reading of the proceedings leaves one with the distinct impression that the Western Powers tired of the matter and must have had some second thoughts about the case which had seemed so promising for their purposes at the outset.

For and Against Tito's Yugoslavia

On July 28, 1948, the government of the Federal People's Republic of Yugoslavia addressed a note to the president of the Security Council, in which it accused the United States and the United Kingdom of violating certain provisions of the peace treaty with Italy, concerning the Free Territory of Trieste.

This area, including the city of Trieste and adjacent territory, was established by the peace treaty with Italy in 1947, which called upon the UN Security Council to select a governor for the territory. However, the Council had been unable to accomplish this task because the Western Powers and the Soviet Union could not agree on a governor who was mutually acceptable. Meanwhile, the Free Territory continued to be administered by Anglo-American (Zone A) and Yugoslav authorities (Zone B). On March 20, 1948, the governments of the United States, Great Britain, and France proposed the return of the whole Trieste territory to Italy. The USSR and Yugoslavia opposed this move.(25)

In its note the Yugoslav government pointed out that the Allied Military Command in Trieste had concluded several agreements with Italy on March 9 and on May 6, 1948, producing the following results: removal of the monetary frontier between the Allied zone of Trieste and Italy, placement of the Anglo-American zone under the financial control of the Italian government, and subordination of the Allied part of the city to Italy, with regard to foreign trade. Stating that Yugoslavia could not "help but associate these violations of independence of the Free Territory of Trieste with the widely known proposal of the three Powers to incorporate the Free Territory of Trieste into Italy," the note requested the Security Council to take steps "for nullifying the respective agreements concluded between the Anglo-American Zone and the Republic of Italy, because by these agreements a situation is created likely to endanger the maintenance of international peace and security."(26) The Yugoslav complaint sparked new debate on Trieste, with the Ukrainian SSR showing a marked interest in its proceedings.

On August 4 the Security Council heard additional information from the Yugoslav delegate, who in substance repeated the charges made in the note. The representatives of the United States and the United Kingdom immediately rejected the charges and then introduced a new element into the discussion, calling attention to the fact that, while their governments periodically submitted reports to the Council on their zone, Yugoslavia had never done so. The French delegate suggested that in order to have a better view of the matter referred to in the Yugoslav note, Yugoslav authorities should also make available a report on their zone.(27)

The delegate of Soviet Ukraine protested against what he considered an attempt on the part of the Western Powers to sidetrack the main issue in the debate. Manuilsky continued, saying that the question of reports, particularly the suggestion of the French representative that the Yugoslav authorities furnish information on their zone, was irrelevant to the point in question. The only matter that should be discussed by the Council was the Yugoslav accusation directed against the American and the British military officials in Trieste who "have for all practical purposes concluded an agreement of the kind envisaged in Article 2 of Annex VI (of the Italian Peace Treaty), which prohibits any attempt at a union placing the Free Territory of Trieste within the bounds of the State of Italy. . . ."(28) Joza Vilfan of Yugoslavia shared the views expressed by Manuilsky.(29)

Supporting the Yugoslav complaint and criticizing the three Western Powers for their plan to return Trieste to Italy, on August 10 Iakov Malik of the Soviet Union stated that the speedy appointment of a governor for the Free Territory, as well as satisfaction of Yugoslav demands, should be the Security Council's goal.(30) The next day Manuilsky continued the Soviet line of argument. Stressing the importance of upholding international treaties and agreements, he noted that

> wherever the view is held that treaties are nothing more than scraps of paper which can be torn up and violated at will by one of the parties, there can be no stable international order, and normal international relations give way to arbitrary methods fraught with serious complications and conflicts.

The communist diplomat then remarked that, although "the articles of the Peace Treaty with Italy concerning the Statute of Trieste were not such as could satisfy the peoples of the Slav countries," the delegation of the Soviet Union had signed the treaty at the Paris peace conference. However, "two years have elapsed since the Peace Conference was held in Paris; yet the decisions relating to Trieste have not been implemented." Specifically, by the unfulfilled decisions Manuilsky meant the failure to appoint a governor for Trieste, for which he blamed the United States and the United Kingdom. Charging these countries with transforming the Free Territory of Trieste "into a sort of mandated territory, used as a naval and military base by the United Kingdom and the United States fleets," Manuilsky told the Council that the Allied command regarded the Free Territory "as its own bailiwick, which can be taken away from some and given to others, in utter disregard of the international Statute of Trieste and treaties concluded on the subject."

Such violations of international agreements were unacceptable to the Ukrainian delegation, particularly since its people "have been taught by Generalissimo Stalin to respect such documents, and all treaties and agreements to which the signature of the Union of Soviet Socialist Republics has been appended." Finally, Manuilsky expressed support for the Yugoslav request that the agreements between the Anglo-American command and the Italian government be invalidated, and he urged the Security Council to deal with the problem of the governorship for Trieste.(31)

On August 16, speaking for the United Kingdom, Cadogan denied the charge that the United States, France, and the United Kingdom were responsible for obstructing such an appointment; he laid the blame for this on the USSR.(32) Then, on August 19, the Yugoslavian representative agreed with both Soviet delegations and blamed all three Western Powers.(33) At the same meeting, the Ukrainian representative, Manuilsky, submitted a draft resolution which read:

> *Having considered* the note of the Government of the Federal People's Republic of Yugoslavia and
> *Considering* that the question of the appointment of a Governor of the Free Territory of Trieste has not yet been settled, and that the delay is making it difficult to implement other provisions of the Peace Treaty with Italy and decisions of the Council of Ministers of Foreign Affairs of 22 April 1947,
> *The Security Council*
> *Considers* that it is urgently necessary to settle the question of the appointment of a Governor of the Free Territory of Trieste.(34)

The United States delegate objected to the Ukrainian proposal on the grounds that it was irrelevant to the subject under discussion — that is to say, the Yugoslav complaint. The Soviet representative, who was also president of the Security Council for August, disagreed and stated that the problem of a governor was of fundamental importance for the solution of the entire Trieste question. Referring to the Ukrainian proposal, Malik observed that, in fact, "this proposal was made by the USSR delegation, while the delegation of the Ukrainian SSR tabled it as a formal resolution." The British delegate shared the misgivings of his American colleague concerning the relevance of the Ukrainian resolution, and stated that, if it were put forward, he would not participate in the vote. In defense of his proposal, Manuilsky pointed out that since the entire debate on the Yugoslav complaint revolved around the Free Territory of Trieste, which still had a temporary status, it was time to put an end to this state of affairs by implementing "one of the fundamental conditions envisaged by the Treaty" — the appointment of a governor. The Ukrainian communist warned the Council that its members "may evade the issue, may abstain, or refuse to vote on this resolution, but by doing so they will be showing that it is they who wish to prolong the abnormal situation which has arisen in Trieste. . . ."(35)

The debate on the Trieste question ended on August 19. On that day, votes were taken on the two resolutions, Yugoslavia's(36) and Ukraine's. The Yugoslav proposal called on the Security Council to annul the agreements between Italy and the Allied authorities in Trieste as being incompatible with the Italian peace treaty. This proposal received only two affirmative votes (USSR and Ukrainian SSR) and was not carried. (Yugoslavia, not being a member of the Council, did not vote). The Ukrainian resolution fared no better, although, besides the two Soviet votes, it obtained the votes of China and Syria. After the defeat of his resolution, Manuilsky evinced his dissatisfaction by declaring that the outcome of the voting on the Ukrainian proposal had demonstrated that a sizable section of the Council adhered to the position of the United States and the United Kingdom, which did not want to abide by the treaty's provisions concerning the Trieste territory. Malik spoke in a similar vein.(37)

It is instructive to note that, in spite of Yugoslavia's expulsion from the Cominform at the end of June 1948 — the famous Stalin-Tito break,(38) the delegations of Ukraine and the USSR steadfastly supported the Yugoslav position in the Trieste dispute. The reason for this action is readily discernible. Moscow was well aware that, Tito's heresies notwithstanding, Yugoslavia was still a communist country, and in the struggle for power and influence in the world, the Western capitalist states were the main enemy. Soviet grand strategy required weakening of the Western camp, especially its strongest members, the United States and Great Britain. The Yugoslav complaint (meant to discredit Anglo-American policies in their zone) thus was one means to that end.

While siding with the Yugoslav position, the Ukrainian delegation introduced a resolution which, although outwardly pro-Yugoslav and anti-Western, seemed to have a distinct purpose of its own. In fact, its aim had no connection with the Yugoslav note which contained not a single word about a governor for Trieste. Basing itself on a strong legal point, the Ukrainian proposal, if implemented, would in all probability have meant the withdrawal of both the Western Powers and Yugoslavia from the Free Territory of Trieste. Such a development might have been welcomed by the Kremlin leadership, which perhaps would have gained from an arrangement making the strategic area of Trieste neutral ground, free from both Anglo-American and Yugoslav influence. Leaving aside American and British intentions in the region, it was no secret that Belgrade coveted at least a part of the Trieste territory, and the departure of its troops and officials from the Yugoslav zone could have been regarded as a blow to Tito's prestige. Thus, while the Soviets on the one hand supported the Yugoslav position in the Trieste dispute, they also simultaneously tried to undermine Yugoslav influence in the area.

Ukrainian participation in the Trieste controversy did not end with the rejection of its resolution in August 1948. In a letter dated February 8, 1949, addressed to the president of the Security Council, the representative of the Soviet Union again brought up the matter of the appointment of a governor. The Council discussed the problem on February 17 and 21, March 28, and May 10.(39)

The delegate of the Ukrainian SSR spoke at all meetings. On February 21 Tarasenko reminded the Council of the Ukrainian proposal of August 1948 and repeated the familiar charges against the United States and the United Kingdom concerning the appointment of a governor:

> Now what is behind this violation by the Governments of the United States of America and the United Kingdom on the part of the Peace Treaty with Italy which deals with the appointment of a Governor of Trieste? There is no doubt that the main reason is the desire of the United States of America and the United Kingdom indefinitely to prolong the occupation of the Territory for the advancement of the United States plans for military and economic expansion.

He expressed his support of the USSR resolution.(40) On March 28 and on May 10, Tarasenko continued his criticism of the Western Powers, including France, for their unwillingness to choose a governor. Accusing these states of "a crude unilateral violation of international obligations," he pointed out that "the United States and the United Kingdom Governments began by failing to fulfill their international obligations under the Yalta and Potsdam Agreements, and now a new instance has been added in connection with the Peace Treaty with Italy." He told these governments to stop sabotaging the appointment of a governor and urged the Council to settle the matter.(41)

When the vote was taken on the Soviet resolution on May 10, it was easily defeated; only two votes were cast in favor, the USSR and the Ukrainian SSR,(42) two votes less than the number obtained for a similar Ukrainian proposal in 1948. By 1949, even more so than in 1948, the leading Western Powers were opposed to appointing any governor for Trieste because they were against the very existence of the Free Territory of Trieste itself. Their official policy stand urged the return of that vital area to Italy, since by that time the Italian government had proved to be pro-Western, and the stigma of an enemy state had all but disappeared. Had the Kremlin agreed to a governor in 1947 or in the early months of 1948, the territory of Trieste might have existed, free or otherwise, to the present day. However, during this time, Tito apparently was still considered orthodox, and his territorial ambitions had to be defended, if not encouraged. The Stalin-Tito split obviously created new "objective" conditions and the previous policy had to be changed. But it was too late. The subsequent solution of the Trieste problem — the partition of the Free Territory between Italy and Yugoslavia(43) — must have been cold comfort for Soviet foreign policy.

Footnotes

(1) Article 2 (4) of the UN Charter says that "all Members shall refrain in their international relations from the threat or use of force against the territorial integrity or political independence of any state, or in any other manner inconsistent with the Purposes of the United Nations."

(2) Security Counil, *Records,* Third Year, Supplement for January, February and March 1948 (Doc. S/696), 34-37. Also see *The New York Times,* March 11, 1948, p. 2. Concerning events of February 1948 in Czechoslovakia, see Hubert Ripka, *Czechoslovakia Enslaved: The Story of the Communist Coup d'Etat* (London: Gollancz, 1950); Josef Korbel, *The Communist Subversion of Czechoslovakia, 1938-1948* (Princeton: Princeton University Press, 1959). For an opposing communist view, see Vesioly Indrtikh, *Khronika febral'skikh dnei 1948 g v Czekhoslovakii* (Moscow: Gosudarstvennoe izdatel'stvo politicheskoi literatury, 1960); *Istoriia Chekhoslovakii,* Vol. III (Moscow: Izdatel'stvo Akademii Nauk SSR, 1960).

(3) According to the Czechoslovak *charge d'affaires* in Washington, Jan Papenk was dismissed from his post on March 10, apparently after submitting the complaint (see *The New York Times,* March 14, 1948).

(4) Security Council, *Records,* Third Year, Supplement for January, February and March 1948 (Doc. S 694), 31-34. Also see *The New York Times,* March 13, 1948, p. 1. Chile was not a member of the Security Council.

(5) Security Council, *Records,* Third Year, No. 36-51, 268th meeting, March 17, 1948, 96-97; Gromyko's statement, *ibid.,* 90-93.

(6) *Ibid.,* 101-102. At one point in the debate, the representative of France compared the present case with the Ukrainian complaint concerning the Greek question. Since the Ukrainian communication was included in the agenda at that time, he saw no reason why the Security Council "should not take the same decision today" (*ibid.,* 98).

(7) *Ibid.,* 102.

(8) *Ibid.,* 102-110.

(9) *Ibid.,* 272nd meeting, March 22, 1948, 175-191.

(10) *Ibid.,* 196-198.

(11) *Ibid.,* 199-203. Taking an anti-Soviet stand on the Czechoslovak matter, the next day the delegate from the United States said, "The representative of

the Ukrainian Soviet Socialist Republic devoted all of his discourse to an attempt to draw a red herring across the whole situation by making a mass of unsubstantiated and fanciful allegations about the conduct of others, some of which were directed toward my Government. This did not help to determine the question now before the Security Council'' (*ibid.*, 273rd meeting, March 23, 1948, 225).

(12) *Ibid.*, 276th meeting, March 31, 1948, 254-271.

(13) See the statement of the British delegate (*ibid.*, 272nd meeting, March 22, 1948, 191-196), and that of the French delegate (*ibid.*, 273rd meeting, March 23, 1948, 206-208).

(14) The British diplomat told the Security Council that ''what happened this last month in Czechoslovakia had happened before in Romania, Bulgaria, Albania, Hungary and Poland.''

(15) Security Council, *Records*, Third Year, 276th meeting, March 31, 1948, 278-284.

(16) *Ibid.*, 284-285.

(17) See the speech by the American delegate, Warren Austin (*ibid.*, No. 56, 281st meeting, April 12, 1948, 25-33).

(18) *Ibid.*, No. 63, 288th meeting, April 29, 1948, 2-13.

(19) *Ibid.*, 13-15.

(20) *Ibid.*, 15.

(21) *Ibid.*, 15-16.

(22) *Ibid.*, 17-18. It was submitted by the Chilean delegate at the 281st meeting on April 12, 1948 (*ibid.*, No. 56, 281st meeting, April 12, 1948, 2).

(23) Actually, the representative of Chile did not propose the number of members in the subcommittee. The number of three was added by the delegate of Argentina (*ibid.*, No. 63, 288th meeting, April 29, 1948, 19).

(24) *Ibid.*, No. 73, 303rd meeting, May 24, 1948, 1-29.

(25) On the problem of Trieste, see Jean-Baptiste Duroselle, *Le conflit de Trieste, 1943-1954* (Brussels: Institut sociologique de l'Universite Libre de Bruxelles, 1966); and Bogdan C. Novak, *Trieste, 1941-1954: The Ethnic, Political and Ideological Struggle* (Chicago: University of Chicago Press, 1970).

(26) Security Council, *Records*, Third Year, Supplement for August 1948 (Doc. S/927), 78-84.

(27) *Ibid.*, No. 101, 344th meeting, August 4, 1948, 2-13.

(28) *Ibid.*, 14-16.

(29) *Ibid.*, 19-20. In a lengthy, elaborate statement on August 10, the American delegate, Philip C. Jessup, maintained that the agreements concluded between the Allied Military Government for Trieste and Italy did not violate the Italian peace treaty. In turn he accused the Yugoslav government of attempting ''to incorporate the Yugoslav Zone directly into Yugoslavia, submitting the population to an alien and totalitarian system. . . .'' Jessup told the United Nations that his government, and also the governments of the United Kingdom and France, were dissatisfied with the treaty and had proposed its revision ''with a view to setting aside the now demonstrably unworkable settlement envisaged in the treaty and arranging for the return of the entire area of the Free Territory of Trieste to Italian sovereignty.'' Such a solution, maintained the American delegate, would be just, but in the meantime the United States would regard the treaty as binding (*ibid.*, No. 102, 345th meeting, August 10, 1948, 2-19).

(30) *Ibid.*, 27-40.

(31) *Ibid.*, No. 103, 348th meeting, August 13, 1948, 2-6.
(32) *Ibid.*, No. 104, 350th meeting, August 16, 1948, 1-4.
(33) *Ibid.*, No. 107, 353rd meeting, August 19, 1948, 6.
(34) *Ibid.*, 18-19. The ''decisions of the Council of Ministers of Foreign Affairs of 22 April 1947,'' reached in Moscow, dealt with the various problems concerning the administration of Trieste.
(35) *Ibid.*, 22-24.
(36) The Yugoslav resolution was proposed on August 13. *Ibid.*, No. 103, 348th meeting, August 13, 1948, 14.
(37) *Ibid.*, No. 107, 354th meeting, August 19, 1948, 36-39.
(38) See Hamilton Fish Armstrong, *Tito and Goliath* (New York: Macmillan, 1951); and Vladimir Dedijer, *The Battle Stalin Lost: Memoirs of Yugoslavia, 1948-1953* (New York: Grosset and Dunlap, 1971).
(39) *Yearbook*, 1948-1949, 315. On February 17 Malik submitted a Soviet resolution which called on the Security Council ''to appoint Colonel Fluckiger as Governor of the Free Territory of Trieste'' (Security Council, *Records*, Fourth Year, No. 14, 411th meeting, February 17, 1949, 14-15). Colonel Herman Fluckiger was at one time Swiss minister to Moscow and his candidacy for governor appears to have been proposed by the British in 1947; however, nothing came of this proposal, since the members of the Security Council could not reach an agreement.
(40) Security Council, *Records*, Fourth Year, No. 15, 412th meeting, February 21, 1949, 2-5.
(41) *Ibid.*, No. 27, 424th meeting, May 10, 1949, 8-9.
(42) *Ibid.*, 9-10.
(43) See Norman Kogan, *A Political History of Postwar Italy* (New York: Praeger, 1966), pp. 86-87.

CHAPTER 7
IN QUEST OF ATOMIC DISARMAMENT
Ukraine versus the Baruch Plan

The Ukrainian delegation was actively engaged in the disarmament debate, which proved to be one of the most important, controversial, and protracted issues faced by the United Nations. The disarmament question concerned itself primarily with the elimination of atomic weapons and the reduction of conventional armaments. This chapter deals with the participation of the Ukrainian SSR in the atomic weapons controversy.

The Atomic Energy Commission (AEC) was unanimously created by the first resolution of the UN General Assembly on January 24, 1946. The initiative to sponsor the resolution came from the governments of the United States, United Kingdom, USSR, Canada, France, and China. There was concern over the destructive power of atomic energy — that is atomic bombs — which had first been used by the United States against Japan, in August 1945. The AEC's "terms of reference," as specified by the General Assembly resolution, were *inter alia,* to "proceed with the outmost despatch and enquire into all phases of the problem (discovery of atomic energy), and make such recommendations from time to time with respect to them as it finds possible"; to "make specific proposals: . . . (b) for control of atomic energy to the extent necessary to ensure its use only for peaceful purposes; (c) for the elimination from national armaments of atomic weapons and of all other major weapons adaptable to mass destruction, . . ." The resolution stipulated that the AEC present reports and make recommendations to the Security Council and that it "be composed of one representative from each of those States represented on the Security Council, and Canada when that State is not a member of the Security Council."

The first meeting of the AEC took place on June 14, 1946, at which time Bernard Baruch, representing the United States, proposed the establishment of an International Atomic Development Authority (IADA) charged with the supervision of atomic energy. The American proposal, which came to be known as the Baruch Plan, called for strict international control of all phases of atomic development. IADA was to own and manage all instruments of the production of nuclear energy; only it would have the right to carry on research in the field of atomic explosives. In other fields of atomic activities, research would be done only by nations who were granted permission by IADA. All countries would allow IADA to inspect locations it considered required inspection, and all those who violated the rights of the authority would be immediately punished. With the veto power of the permanent members of the Security Council in mind, Baruch pointed out that "there must be no veto to protect those who violate their solemn agreements not to develop or use atomic energy for destructive pürposes." After the creation of viable international control, the manufacture of atomic weapons would discontinue and the existing nuclear stockpiles would be eliminated.

Five days later, at the second meeting of the AEC, Gromyko introduced the Soviet proposals. Briefly stated, the Soviet plan envisaged an international convention that would prohibit production as well as use of atomic weapons, and, within a three-month period after its creation, all nuclear weapons would be destroyed. Violation of the convention would be punished by the signatories' domestic legislations; this international agreement would become valid when approved by the Security Council and ratified by its permanent members.

Comparing the American and the Soviet positions even at this early stage shows an impasse: while Washington stressed the importance of international control over atomic energy, an accomplishment that had to be achieved before prohibition and destruction of nuclear arms, Moscow insisted on a reversal of these priorities — accomplishment of the probhition and elimination of nuclear weapons before establishment of the machinery for international control. These divergent positions reflected the existing nuclear situation of the two countries. The United States, since it already possessed atomic weapons, was quite reluctant to lose them unless given a guarantee that no other state would ever produce (and use) them. The USSR, on the other hand, having no nuclear arms and thus being at a great disadvantage vis-a-vis the U.S. wanted tc abolish the American atomic monopoly by proposing to get rid of it altogether.

Both the Baruch Plan and the Soviet counterplan served as a starting point of long and arduous discussions. While the AEC had been deadlocked for some time in its effort to find a compromise between the two views, the General Assembly, on December 14, 1946, unanimously passed a resolution — initiated by the Soviet Union — to regulate and reduce armaments and armed forces. Among other things, the resolution called for "the expeditious fulfillment by the Atomic Energy Commission of its terms of reference." That goal proved to be unattainable; three reports submitted by the AEC to the Security Council showed that. The first report, issued in December 1946 and supported by the commission's majority of ten votes for, with two abstentions (the USSR and Poland), basically embodied the provisions of the Baruch Plan; it recommended the principles for a strong international system of control. A second report, issued in September 1947, which received a vote of 10 for, one against (USSR) and one abstention (Poland), was in some ways a continuation of the first one. It dealt with specific measures for the functions and powers of an international control agency. The third report, passed on May 17, 1948, by a vote of nine to two (the USSR and the Ukrainian SSR voting against), endorsed the principles of the two previous reports, and, after admitting the commission's inability to bridge the gulf between the majority viewpoint and the Soviets, recommended the suspension of its work. In June 1948 the Security Council discussed the third report at several meetings. At one of the meetings, on June 11, the American representative proposed a resolution that, approved the third report's suggestion to suspend deliberation of the AEC.(1)

On June 22, 1948, delegate Manuilsky attacked the United States' proposal for suspending the work of the AEC — such a step was, he declared, "designed to wreck the General Assembly resolutions of 24 January and 14 December 1946 on the exclusion of atomic weapons from national armaments." Since the commission began its work, Manuilsky continued, its meetings showed clearly that the United States was neither willing to prohibit atomic weapons nor to have established a control that would ensure the peaceful uses of atomic energy. The head of the Ukrainian delegation charged "official United States circles" with a desire to retain their atomic weapons monopoly in order to exert pressure on other countries. Furthermore, he pointed out that

> in fact, the policy of the leading circles of the United States in atomic matters was a component part of their concept of world domination, just as the organization of various military and air bases in various parts of the world, the Truman doctrine, the Marshall plan, the policy in Greece and China, and the systematic violation of the United Nations Charter, were separate links of that concept which is threatening the peace of the world. This claim to world domination is also reflected in the United States plan for the establishment of so-called control over atomic energy, now submitted to the Security Council for approval.

The communist diplomat voiced his displeasure over the American plan to create an international agency or trust to control atomic energy. "Under the guise of an international control organ" the United States would actually dominate this field and would also impose its will on the economies of other countries. Such an international trust, which would be "over and above the United Nations," might even result in the management of the domestic affairs of states. "At one of the Security Council's meetings, this kind of trust was described as a model for a universal world government. May fate preserve the nations from such world government."

Manuilsky blamed Washington and its followers for the failure of the AEC to resolve the problem of atomic energy and warned that this would increase international tension. Criticizing the Baruch Plan for not being compatible with the UN Charter because it endangered "the principle of the equality of large and small States" and violated national sovereignty, he observed that only the Soviet Union had contributed to the realization of the General Assembly resolutions of January 24 and December 14, 1946, by its proposals of June 19, 1946, and June 11, 1947. In conclusion, the Ukrainian representative stated that he could not agree to the American plan of control over atomic energy and that he supported the Soviet position on this subject.(2)

At the same meeting a vote was taken on the United States resolution which called for approval of specific sections of three reports submitted by the UN AEC to the Security Council and also suggested that Secretary-General Lie was to transmit these reports to the General Assembly. Both the USSR and the Ukrainian SSR opposed the resolution, and, since it was of a substantive matter, the Soviet veto barred its adoption.(3) However, the Canadian proposal that the secretary-general transmit the three reports to the General Assembly was adopted, with Ukraine and the Soviet Union abstaining.(4)

Since it was impossible to reach agreement on the control of atomic energy and the prohibition of atomic weapons in either the AEC or the Security Council, it was then up to the General Assembly and its subsidiary organs to try to resolve the difficulty. On October 4, 1948, in Paris, at the meeting of the First Committee of the General Assembly, the Ukrainian foreign minister continued his uncompromising line of reasoning, supporting the USSR resolution and opposing Canada's.(5) Manuilsky said that

> under the terms of the Canadian draft resolution, the First Committee would sanction a situation which would give the United States a free hand in the preparation of a new war and the United Nations would be used to conceal the plans of American reactionary circles.

The Soviet resolution, on the other hand, offered a new basis for the solution of the problem of atomic energy. Manuilsky expressed regret over "the intransigent attitude" displayed by the American delegation in the AEC and contrasted it with the benevolent attitude of Soviet representatives.(6)

Because the several resolutions submitted to the First Committee required careful study, it was decided to establish a subcommittee to deal with the problem. Created on October 7, the subcommittee was to try to reach agreement on a proposal to be presented to the First Committee. It consisted of eleven members "in accordance with the principle of equitable geographical distribution," among them the representatives of the USSR, the Ukrainian SSR, and the United States.(7) After some deliberation, the subcommittee reported to the First Committee that its members had failed to find common agreement on the matter. Instead of one resolution, three were presented in the report — draft resolutions by the Canadians, the Soviets, and the Indians.(8) The report was discussed from October 18 to October 20 at four meetings of the First Committee.

Both Malik and Manuilsky attacked the Canadian proposal. Malik pointed out that

> the Canadian resolution implied the approval of the United States plan by the General Assembly. On that basis, the United States would step up its efforts to impose upon the world a plan which would solve neither the problem of prohibition, nor that of effective control. Quite on the contrary, the reactionary circles in the United States would boost the production of atomic bombs, and fear of war would increase.(9)

For Manuilsky, adoption of the Canadian proposal would have meant the victory of the United States plan; this, he believed, would have resulted in an intolerable international situation for many nations besides the Soviet Union.

> The consequences of adoption of the Baruch Plan affected many peoples and nations besides the USSR. All raw material sources and industrial production of atomic energy would be under the control of an international agency in which United States financial interests would predominate, thus bringing to fruition the dream of Hitler's Germany to place a monopoly of weapons in the hands of a master State while disarming all others.

Manuilsky said that "one group of States" (meaning the Soviet bloc), was defending by its opposition to the Baruch Plan, not only its own interests and rights, but also the interests and rights of medium-size and small states. Manuilsky used the term "new humanism" to describe that which was defended by the Soviet camp.(10)

At the previous meeting, the United States representative stated that the Canadian resolution was the plan "supported by fourteen States which had served on the Atomic Energy Commission, and was opposed by three States only — the USSR, the Ukrainian SSR and Poland."(11) While not denying that statement, Manuilsky nevertheless denied its implication. He pointed out that the plan approved by the majority of states or votes did not mean the support of the majority of the population.

> . . . Mr. Manuilsky remarked that the Eastern European States with only four to six votes had a population equal to those of the United States, Central and Latin America (!) combined, which had twenty-one votes. Furthermore, a survey of the United States public opinion showed that almost half of the people of the United States knew nothing of United States policy on control of atomic energy. Mr. Manuilsky inferred that even less was known about it in Latin America.(12)

When it was put to a vote, the First Committee rejected both the Soviet and Indian proposals, and the slightly revised Canadian resolution was adopted by an overwhelming majority.(13) The matter was then submitted to the General Assembly, which considered it on November 3 and 4 at the plenary sessions.

In the General Assembly the battle lines were drawn as before, and no compromise was reached between majority and minority viewpoints. Led by the United States, Britain, and Canada, the majority defended the Canadian draft resolution adopted by the First Committee. The minority — Communist block countries, the Ukrainian SSR, Belorussian SSR, Poland, Czechoslovakia, and Yugoslavia — criticized it. They viewed the Soviet proposal, rejected by the First Committee, as the only practical solution to the long-drawn out atomic dispute.

Manuilsky was the last delegate to speak on the subject. He chose to comment on the statements of the other representatives, and he dwelt on the faults and virtues of the Canadian and the Soviet resolutions, respectively. Manuilsky told the General Assembly that "the question of prohibition of atomic weapons and the establishment of control of atomic energy was of supreme importance for the maintenance of international peace, security and cooperation." He further argued that failure to come to any understanding on the atomic problem divided the world "into the opposing forces of reaction (the Western countries, particularly the United States and the United Kingdom) and war, on the one hand, and peace and progress on the other." The Ukrainian foreign minister rhetorically asked what might happen to those countries accepting this plan, and told the assembled representatives that they would lose their economic and political independence and sovereignty. Criticizing those delegates who allegedly regarded the principle of national sovereignty as being obsolete, Manuilsky presented the Soviet government as its ardent defender.

Manuilsky accused the Anglo-American bloc of putting an end to the activities of the Atomic Energy Commission and charged the authors of the Canadian proposal with delaying tactics in the resumption of its work. He said that the United States was producing more atomic bombs "while at the same time trying to deceive world public opinion with regard to the sincerity of its desire for peace." The Anglo-American bloc also rejected the USSR resolution, submitted in the First Committee, in spite of the fact that it "disposed of one of the fundamental differences that had separated the USSR and the United States for two and a half years." Manuilsky then proceeded to defend the Soviet Union's position on the control of the production of nuclear energy as well as the problem of sanctions against those states which might violate agreements dealing with the prohibition of atomic weapons and the control of atomic energy.(14)

Following Manuilsky's speech, the General Assembly voted first on the Soviet resolution, previously rejected by the First Committee. The result was 6 votes in favor, 40 votes against, and 5 abstentions. The proposal submitted by the First Commitee (the revised Canadian resolution) was adopted (with 40 votes in favor, 6 votes against, and 4 abstentions).(15)

After some two and one-half years of intense, often acrimonious debates over the disposition of potentially man's most dangerous invention, no solution could be found to satisfy the opposing sides. The seeming Soviet concession, referred to by Manuilsky, was to create two simultaneous conventions, one to deal with the prohibition of nuclear weapons and the other with the international control of atomic energy. This might have been interpreted as a retreat from the previous position, stressing the priority of prohibition, but it did not impress the West. After all, the USSR and its allies were still opposed to the three reports approved by the majority of the AEC, which emphasized control before prohibition. The November victory in the General Assembly for the United States and the majority of the Assembly's members was clear enough, but since one of the world's two leading powers chose not to include itself in this company, the victory was essentially meaningless.

As the actions of the Ukrainian delegation in 1948 unmistakably attested, the question of nuclear energy and weapons was primarily a political one. The nature of postwar confrontation between the United States and the Soviet Union constituted a power struggle, and the atomic controversy was part of it. Observing the Ukrainian SSR attack the United States for its nuclear policies (the Baruch Plan), one hardly could have thought that it was the same plan which was to trade possession of an "absolute" weapon for American and world security. The country that wanted to give up the deadliest instrument of war — an event unique in history — was accused of trying to dominate the world. The Baruch Plan stipulated some limitations on soveriegnty of states, but to say that such a step would mean the loss of economic and political independence was purely propagandistic. To be sure, this propaganda could not have been very effective, for it came from one whose government's claim to economic as well as political independence and sovereignty was rather precarious, and therefore the righteous exhortations of its communist spokesmen could not but generate suspicion or even contempt. On the other hand, to support the Soviet proposals, which amounted to unilateral disarmament by the United States, was to invite inevitable failure while successfully prolonging the debate and marking time until the day when the USSR would also have nuclear arms.

The resolution adopted by the General Assembly on November 4, 1948, urged the AEC to renew its activities(16) in order to break the deadlock between the two opposing camps on the international control of atomic energy and the prohibition of nuclear weapons. The commission and its working committee held several meetings in 1949, during which the delegation of the Ukrainian SSR maintained its previous position.

On March 22, 1949, Tarasenko of the Ukrainian SSR criticized the General Assembly's resolution of November 4, 1948, as being inadequate for the AEC's purposes, since it departed from the original task of the commission, as assigned to it by the Assembly's 1946 resolutions of January 24 and December 14. The Ukrainian delegate insisted that the basic goal of these two proposals was the "prohibition of the use of atomic energy for military purposes" and that the AEC was to carry out its work accordingly. Unfortunately, he stated, because of the attitude of the U.S. and the United Kingdom, this fundamental question was not being pursued. As the three reports of the commission had shown, it "merely confined itself to an investigation of methods which would enable the United States to strengthen its monopoly of the production and use of atomic energy" as well as "finding arguments in justification of the use of atomic energy by the United States for military purposes.'' Tarasenko then charged the Anglo-American majority with an attempt to terminate the work of the AEC.

> It was only under the pressure of world opinion, and because of the concern shown by a number of delegations at the first part of the third session of the General Assembly, that the United States and the United Kingdom delegations were compelled to agree to the adoption of an additional paragraph recommending that the Atomic Energy Commission should resume its work. The whole tenor of the resolution, however, limits the Atomic Energy Commission's activities in advance, leaving it to deal with third-rate and unimportant questions.

Tarasenko regarded such a situation as intolerable and suggested that the resolution submitted by the Soviet Union delegation in the AEC would resolve the difficulty.(17)

However, the difficulty was not resolved, nor was there even a real chance for resolution, because a similar Soviet resolution had already been rejected. In the Atomic Energy Commission the two positions remained frozen: the viewpoint of the majority which followed the General Assembly resolution of November 4 versus the USSR and the Ukrainian SSR which had voted against that resolution and now were trying to circumvent it. The deadlock existed, but it took several meetings of the commission and of its working committee to end further futile deliberations.(18)

On July 29, at what proved to be the last meeting of the AEC,(19) the majority (in a nine to two vote) adopted the American resolution, an act which openly illustrated the incompatibility of Soviet and Western views with regard to the international control of atomic energy and the prohibition of nuclear weapons. After stating that ''the Atomic Energy Commission has surveyed its programme of work in order to determine whether further work would be practicable and useful,'' the American resolution noted that the Soviet Union and the Ukrainian SSR continued to oppose the General Assembly proposal of November 4, 1948, while at the same time insisting upon the acceptance of the Soviet resolution, which had been defeated by the General Assembly on that same day. The United States resolution further said that the USSR recommendations, since they provided ''for national ownership, operation and management of dangerous atomic facilities,'' would not solve the existing difficulty; instead, they ''would render ineffective the prohibition of atomic weapons, and would continue dangerous national rivalries in the field of atomic energy.'' Finally, the resolution emphasized the uselessness of discussions in the AEC ''until such time as the sponsoring Powers have reported that there exists a basis for agreement."(20)

On September 15 and 16 the Security Council considered the two resolutions adopted by the AEC. The Canadian representative was of the opinion that the Council should not discuss these resolutions at length but should merely forward them to the General Assembly. He pointed out that the six sponsoring powers had begun their deliberations and it would be advisable to wait for their report to the Assembly in order to have a more meaningful dialogue and he submitted a procedural resolution to that effect.(21)

The two Soviet representatives had a different view about the course of action to be followed in the Security Council. In a lengthy statement, Manuilsky pursued the well-trodden path of repetitive Soviet pronouncements on the subject. He told his listeners that it was "simply astounding" that such resolutions, which contradicted the General Assembly proposals of January 24 and December 14, 1946, could have been produced by the Anglo-American bloc:

> The challenge to world public opinion which is indicated by the submission of such resolutions as those now before us can be explained only by the fact that the ruling circles of the United States have had their judgment shaken and have come to believe that they can really lay down the law to the whole world.
> It will be remembered that others have acted with the same presumption in the past and that it led to no good.

The Ukrainian diplomat defended the stand taken by the USSR and the Ukrainian SSR in the atomic dispute and urged that the AEC continue its work.(22)

Manuilsky's speech was followed by that of the Soviet Union representative, Semeon Tsarapkin, who said essentially the same thing. He submitted a resolution which, at least in part, tried to annul the two AEC proposals of July 29 and emasculate the Canadian proposal.(23) The final outcome of this brief Security Council debate, which saw almost no participation on the part of the non-Soviet majority, brought defeat to the Soviet resolution,(24) while the amended Canadian proposal was adopted. Surprisingly enough, the amendment to the Canadian proposal was offered by Manuilsky, and since it was of minor importance, it was readily accepted by the Canadian delegate.(25)

The General Assembly then referred the subject of atomic controversy to the Ad Hoc Political Committee, which held several meetings in November to deal with the problem; however, no progress was made toward reconciling the differences between the two opposing sides.(26) An atomic explosion set off by the Soviet Union in September(27) did not help matters, for it became obvious that the United States' nuclear monopoly was ended, and that the USSR, proud of its recent achievement, would more than ever hold to a point of view incompatible with that of the majority.

In the Ad Hoc Political Committee, Manuilsky duly stressed the significance of the Soviet Union's ''possession of the secret of atomic energy production,'' but he was careful to observe that such a development did not diminish the USSR's efforts toward the prohibition of atomic weapons and establishment of international control over nuclear energy. Manuilsky said that, while the Soviet Union endeavored to utilize the energy for ''peaceful and constructive benefits for all peoples,'' the United States had ''repeatedly demonstrated its desire to use atomic energy exclusively for military purposes in order to consolidate and expand the power of its monopolies.'' He charged some groups in the U.S. with the intent of subjecting the USSR to an atomic bombardment; he derided those who considered the atomic bomb as an absolute weapon against which all defense was useless. Manuilsky also stated that ''as early as September 1946, Generalissimo Stalin had discounted the absolute effects of the atomic weapon and had confidently predicted that the monopoly of the bomb could not exist for long and that its use would be prohibited.'' The Ukrainian delegate regretted that the new situation in the nuclear debate, whichcame as a result of the atomic explosion in the Soviet Union, had not altered the attitude of the Anglo-American bloc, which still held to the Baruch Plan. He opposed the Canadian-French resolution and supported the one submitted by the USSR.(28)

On November 14 (the last meeting devoted to the problem), the majority of the Ad Hoc Political Committee adopted the revised Canadian French proposal and rejected the Soviet resolution.(29) The result was the same in the General Assembly: the resolution recommended by the Ad Hoc Political Cmmittee received overwhelming endorsement, but the Soviet proposal already defeated in the committee again failed to be adopted.(30) In terms of General Assembly votes, the Western view prevailed, but the nuclear controversy was not resolved.

Throughout the atomic dispute in the AEC, the Soviet Union pursued a lonely road, supported only by Poland (1946-1947) and by the Ukrainian SSR (1948-1949). Under such circumstances, the role of the Ukrainian delegation should not be underestimated. True enough, the presence of Ukrainian representatives was not decisive, for the Soviet delegation still found itself in an uncomfortable minority. Nevertheless, another friendly vote and especially additional participation in the debate was a welcome relief and made even defeat more palatable.

Of all the cases discussed thus far in this study (with the possible exception of the one dealing with Czechoslovakia), the question of atomic disarmament and control of nuclear energy was, for Moscow, of greatest import. After successfully meeting the German challenge and apparently emerging from the war as one of the leading world powers, the USSR was suddenly confronted with still another menace, the atomic bomb. While no amount of discussion in the United Nations could have removed this threat had Washington chosen to solve the communist problem by forceful means, the opportunity to discredit the nuclear policy of its chief political rival in the forum of an international organization was not overlooked by the Kremlin. Here, then, the Ukrainian delegates made their contributions, and it is instructive to observe that at times Manuilsky spoke as if he was the representative of the Soviet Union and not merely of the Ukrainian SSR.(31)

The Ukrainian foreign minister — as well as other representatives of the Soviet bloc — spoke with understandable pride about the USSR's success in ending the American atomic monopoly. Stalin was correct; the monopoly had not lasted long. Now that the Soviets were capable of producing nuclear weapons, the era of fruitless atomic disarmament negotiations would be succeeded by a perilous nuclear arms race. While the delegates of the Soviet Union and Ukraine fought their verbal battles in the Atomic Energy Commission, in the Security Council, and in other organs of the United Nations, Moscow had been quitely working to manufacture the bomb. Once that was achieved, the Soviet Union's lack of parity with the U.S. disappeared.(32)

Footnotes

(1) See *Yearbook* 1946-1947, 64-66, 444-451; and *Yearbook,* 1947-1948, 461-473. Also see *The United Nations and Disarmament, 1945-1965* (New York: United Nations Office of Public Information, 1967), pp. 11-21; and Joseph I. Lieberman, *The Scorpion and the Tarantula: The Struggle to Control Atomic Weapons, 1945-1949* (Boston: Houghton Mifflin, 1970). For a discussion of Soviet views on this question, see A. G. Mileikovskii, ed., *Mezhdunarodnye otnosheniia posle Vtoroi Mirovoi Voiny,* Vol. I (Moscow: Gosudarstvennoe izdatel'stvo politicheskoi literatury, 1962), pp. 549-564.

(2) Security Council, *Records,* Third Year, No. 88, 325th meeting, June 22, 1948, 2-8.

(3) *Ibid.,* 11-12.

(4) *Ibid.,* 19-20.

(5) Both resolutions were presented in the First Committee. The Soviet proposal called for continuation of the work in the Security Council and in the AEC as spelled out by the General Assembly resolutions of January 24 and December 14, 1946, and urged the members of the Security Council and AEC "to prepare a draft convention on the prohibition of atomic weapons and a draft convention on the establishment of effective international control over atomic energy, to be signed and brought into operation simultaneously" (United

Nations, General Assembly, *First Committee, Official Records,* Third Session of the General Assembly, Part I, Annexes to the Summary Records of Meetings, 1948 (Paris, Palais de Chaillot: 1948) Doc. A/C.1/310 (hereafter cited as General Assembly, *First Committee*). The Canadian proposal was similar to the U.S. resolution, rejected by the negative vote of the USSR on June 22, 1948, in the Security Council (*ibid.,* 3 (Doc. A C1 308)).

(6) *Ibid.,* Summary Records of Meetings, 21 September-8 December 1948, 148th meeting, October 4, 1948, 57-60.

(7) *Ibid.,* Annexes to the Summary Records of Meetings, 1948, 16 (Doc. A/C.1/333).

(8) *Ibid.,* 18-20. The Canadian resolution, adopted by majority vote in the subcommittee, was a revised Canadian resolution first proposed in the First Committee. After suggesting approval of certain parts of the first and second reports of the AEC "as constituting the necessary basis for establishing an effective system of international control of atomic energy," the proposal expressed concern at the failure of finding agreement in the atomic dispute; it then requested the six countries, which sponsored the resolution of January 24, 1946, in the General Assembly to try "to determine when there exists a basis for agreements on the international control of atomic energy to ensure its use only for peaceful purposes and for elimination from national armaments of atomic weapons, and thereupon to request the Secretary-General to reconvene the Atomic Energy Commission, . . . in order to resume its task, which is to prepare for submission to the Security Council, as early as possible, treaties on convention or conventions incorporating the Commission's ultimate proposals." The Soviet resolution, rejected by the subcommittee, was the same as the one put forward in the First Committee. The Indian proposal was a simplified and abbreviated version of the Canadian resolution; it was not adopted in the subcommittee.

(9) *Ibid.,* Summary Records of Meetings, 21 September-8 December 1948, 162nd meeting, October 18, 1948, 177.

(10) *Ibid.*

(11) *Ibid.,* 162nd meeting, October 18, 1948, 169.

(12) *Ibid.,* 163rd meeting, October 18, 1948, 190.

(13) *Ibid.,* 165th meeting, October 20, 1948, 205-208.

(14) General Assembly, *Records,* Third Session, Part I, 157th plenary meeting, November 4, 1948, 461-466.

(15) *Ibid.,* 468-470.

(16) This part of the resolution stated that "*the General Assembly calls upon* the Atomic Energy Commission to resume its sessions, to survey its programme of work, and to proceed to the further study such of the subjects remaining in the programme of work as it considers to be practicable and useful" (General Assembly, *Records,* Third Session, Part I, Annexes to the Summary Records of Meetings, 1948, 275.

(17) United Nations, Atomic Energy Commission, *Official Records,* Fourth Year (New York: Lake Success), No. 4, 20th meeting, March 22, 1949, pp. 2-4 (hereafter cited as AEC, *Records*). The Soviet resolution referred to by Tarasenko was proposed by Malik to the commission on February 25 (*ibid.,* No. 2, 18th meeting, February 25, 1949, 8). In essence, the resolution was almost identical with the USSR proposal rejected by the General Assembly on November 4, 1948. Some of the representatives — for example, Sir Terence

Shone of the United Kingdom — expressed their dissatisfaction with the alleged Soviet practice of resubmitting a resolution previously defeated by the majority in other organs of the UN (*ibid.,* 10).

(18) *Yearbook,* 1948-1949, 352-354.

(19) "The Atomic Energy Commission did not meet again after 29 July, 1949. . . . The commission was dissolved on 11 January, 1952 by General Assembly resolution . . ." (*The United Nations and Disarmament, 1945-1965,* 23-24).

(20) AEC, *Records,* Fourth Year, No. 8, 24th meeting, July 29, 1949, 36-38. At the same meeting another resolution was adopted, which dealt with the Soviet proposal presented to the AEC on February 25 (and other similar USSR proposals). The conclusion of this commission's resolution was that "no useful purpose can be served by further discussions in the Atomic Energy Commission of those (Soviet) proposals which have already been considered and rejected by the appropriate organs of the United Nations" (*ibid.,* 9-10, 16, 23).

(21) Security Council, *Records,* Fourth Year, No. 42, 445th meeting, September 15, 1949, 47-48. The full text of the resolution read, "*The Security Council having received and examined* the letter dated 29 July, 1949 from the chairman of the Atomic Energy Commission transmitting two resolutions (AEC 42 and AEC 43) adopted at the 24th meeting of the Commission on 29 July 1949, *directs* the Secretary-General to transmit this letter and the accompanying resolutions to the General Assembly and to the Member nations of the United Nations."

(22) *Ibid.,* No. 43, 446th meeting, September 16, 1949, 4-11.

(23) *Ibid.,* 11-19. The USSR resolution stated in part that "*the Security Council, . . . requests* the Atomic Energy Commission to continue its work with a view to fulfilling the tasks entrusted to it by the General Assembly resolutions of 24 January and 14 December 1946."

(24) *Ibid.,* No. 43, 447th meeting, September 16, 1949, 28.

(25) *Ibid.,* 23-24. The Ukrainian amendment added several words to the second part of the Canadian resolution. As amended, the second part read, "*Directs* the Secretary-General to transmit this letter and the accompanying resolutions together with a record of the discussion on this question in the Atomic Energy Commission to the General Assembly and to the Member nations of the United Nations" (for the original Canadian resolution, see footnote 21). Both Soviet delegates abstained from voting on the resolution Ukraine amended.

(26) *Yearbook,* 1948-1949, 356-359. Between August 9 and October 13, the six permanent members of the AEC held ten meetings, but no compromise or solution was reached (see General Assembly, *Records,* Fourth Session, 1949, Supplement No. 15 (A/913, A/1045, and A/1050)).

(27) "As the fourth session of the General Assembly got under way in September 1949, the United States announced that the Soviet Union had exploded an atomic bomb, thus becoming the second nuclear Power" (see *The United Nations and Disarmament, 1945-1965,* 23).

(28) *Ad Hoc Political Committee,* Summary Records of Meetings, 27 September-7 December, 1949, 33rd meeting, November 10, 1949, 191-193. In brief, the revised joint resolution presented by Canada and France requested "Governments to do everything in their power to make possible, by the acceptance of effective international control, the effective prohibition and

elimination of nuclear weapons"; requested the permanent members of AEC to hold further talks; proposed that states, "in the use of their rights of sovereignty, join in mutual agreement to limit the individual exercise of those rights in the control of atomic energy to the extent required, . . . for the promotion of world security and peace. . . ." The Soviet proposal, in short, blamed the U.S. and the United Kingdom for failing to implement the General Assembly resolutions of January 24 and December 14, 1946; regarded the consultations between the permanent members of the AEC as not being helpful because of the wrong position taken by the U.S. and the United Kingdom concerning the problem; directed the AEC to return to its task of carrying out the above General Assembly's resolutions and to prepare "a draft convention for the prohibition of atomic weapons and a draft convention for the control of atomic energy, it being understood that both conventions should be concluded and put into effect simultaneously") *Ad Hoc Political Committee,* Annex to the Summary Records of Meetings, Vol. I, 1949, 68-69).

(29) *Ad Hoc Political Committee,* 37th meeting, November 14, 1949, 217-218.

(30) General Assembly, *Records,* 254th plenary meeting, November 23, 1949, 358. Manuilsky was the last speaker before the vote was taken on the resolutions. Fighting against the proposal submitted by the Ad Hoc Political Committee, he said that "the Canadian-French draft resolution was not intended to serve the interests of peace but the interests of such monopolies as the Dupont, Westinghouse and General Electric companies, all of which, under pretext of working for United States national defense, had made the production of atomic weapons one of the most profitable concerns in the United States" (*ibid.,* 354-355).

(31) See Chapter 9 of this study.

(32) Was Ukraine also a member of the exclusive nuclear club? And Belorussia? The question was never raised by Manuilsky with respect to Ukraine, and by no one else in the case of either of these constituent republics of the USSR; futile or not, it is an interesting query.

PART III
FICTION AND REALITY

CHAPTER 8
A SOVEREIGN AND INDEPENDENT UKRAINIAN STATE?
Juridical Riddle

Soviet political leaders, diplomats, and jurists have long maintained that Soviet republics are independent and sovereign states. It was on this basis that Gromyko made his initial request at the Dumbarton Oaks conference to seat sixteen Soviet republics in the projected world organization. At Yalta and at San Francisco, Moscow cited Soviet constitutional amendments of February 1944 as proof that the republics were independent in foreign affairs. However, the entry of only two of the Soviet republics into an international organization posed an obvious inconsistency with the juridical position, for one could legitimately ask why the remaining republics, which possessed the same constitutional rights, were excluded. Prof. Alexander Dallin noted that

> Moscow has apparently not been bothered by the illogical situation that led to the separate membership and dual representation of two republics (by their own missions and by the U.S.S.R.), while the remaining ''sister republics'' — legally on an equal footing with the Ukraine and Byelorussia — have only the Soviet Union as their spokesman.(1)

Since Ukraine is the focus of this study, it is its sovereignty and independence which must be thoroughly examined. But before resolving the status of the sovereignty and independence of the Ukrainian republic, and even more basic question must be posed: is Ukraine a state?(2)

The Ukrainian Soviet Socialist Republic is one of the republics of the Union of Soviet Socialist Republics, described by the Soviet Constitution as a federation.(3) David Zlatopol'skii noted that

> the peculiarity of the USSR as a federal state consists in that its subjects are *sovereign states;* sovereignty of the members of the federation stipulates the principles of their unification in one state and their rights as subjects of the federation.(4) (Italics in the original).

It follows from this that the Ukrainian SSR, despite the fact that it is also a constituent part of the Soviet Union, is a sovereign state. For a legal answer to the question of what ground is there to consider the Ukrainian SSR a state, one must look at both the All-Union and Ukrainian Constitutions.(5)

The first article of the Ukrainian Constitution states that "the Ukrainian Soviet Socialist Republic is a socialist state of workers and peasants." The four constituent elements of statehood are also covered in the Ukrainian Constitution: 1. Territory: referred to in Articles 6, 15, and 18; 2. Citizenry: mentioned in Article 17 and in Chapter VIII, which is entitled "The Basic Rights and Duties of Citizens" (Articles 98-113). 3. State power: asserted in Articles 3 and 19; in Chapter III, "The Highest Organs of State Power of the Ukrainian Soviet Socialist Republic" (Articles 20-38); in Chapter IV, "The Organs of State Administration of the Ukrainian Soviet Socialist Republic" (Articles 39-53); and in Chapter V, "The Local Organs of State Power" (Articles 54-79). 4. The capability of maintaining relations with foreign states: enumerated in Articles 15b, 19zl, 30j, 30k, and 43h. Although the Ukrainian Constitution has essential provisions for statehood, the Ukrainian SSR is nonetheless not a separate entity, but a member of the Soviet "federation." Thus, relevant provisions of the Soviet Union Constitution must also be included in an examination of Ukraine's claim to statehood.

Article 6 of the Soviet Constitution (identical to Article 6 of the Ukrainian Constitution) ascribes all territory of the USSR (including Ukraine) as being the property of the Soviet Union. Such double ownership of land imposes restrictions on the Ukrainian state. Article 21 stipulates that "uniform Union citizenship is established for the citizens of the USSR. Each citizen of the Union Republic is a citizen of the USSR." It follows from this, and is explicitly stated by Article 17 of the Ukrainian Constitution, that a citizen of Ukraine is a citizen of the Soviet Union. The reverse is also true — a citizen of the USSR residing in the territory of the Ukrainian Republic becomes its citizen — as, again, Article 17 of the Ukrainian Constitution declares. Such a fluid nature of the citizenry of the republic, however, does not enhance the permanency of its population, thus contributing instability to one of the essential ingredients of statehood.

In Chapter IV, "The Higher Organs of State Power in the Union Republics." (Articles 57-63), and in Chapter VI, "The Organs of State Administration of the Union Republics" (Articles 79-88), the Soviet Union Constitution speaks of the machinery of government of the republics on their respective territories. However, the constitution also makes it clear that, in addition to the republican governments, there is an All-Union government, whose authority extends to all the Soviet republics. For example, Article 19 says that "the laws of the USSR have the same force on the territory of all Union Republics." Articles 30 and 67 state, respectively, that "the highest organ of state power in the USSR is the Supreme Soviet of the USSR" and that "decisions and orders of the Council of Ministers of the USSR are binding throughout the territory of the USSR." In the case of the Ukrainian SSR, these constitutional provisions mean that there are two legitimate governments in the Ukrainian Republic — for, instead of having one necessary element of statehood of the same nature, Ukraine has two.

Finally, Article 18a provides that "each Union Republic has the right to enter into direct relations with foreign states, to conclude agreements and exchange diplomatic and consular representatives with them." However, this capacity of the republics to conduct foreign relations is circumscribed by that section of Article 14a which ascribes to the jurisdiction of the Union "representation of the USSR in international relations, conclusion, ratification and denunciation of treaties of the USSR with other states..." It is obvious that, since the Soviet republics are integral parts of the USSR, the later, by directing its relations with foreign countries, also directs the external relations of Soviet Union republics. Applied to Ukraine, such a constitutional arrangement spells out the double jurisdiction over the management of its foreign affairs.

Taking into account the stipulations of both the Ukrainian SSR and Soviet Union Constitutions, the Ukrainian SSR seems to be legally a peculiar kind of state, a state *sui generis* (6) within the Soviet-type federation. Obviously, this peculiarity amounts to a legal deficiency.

This raises another question to be resolved: can this type of state be sovereign and independent? Article 13 of the Ukrainian Constitution states, in part, that "outside of Article 14 of the USSR Constitution the Ukrainian Soviet Socialist Republic exercises state power independently, fully preserving its sovereign rights." Article 15 of the Soviet Union Constitution says that "the sovereignty of the Union Republic is limited only in the spheres defined in Article 14 of the Constitution of the USSR. Outside of these spheres each Union Republic exercises state power independently. The USSR protects the sovereign rights of the Union Republics." The significance of Article 14 lies in the fact that, according to it, a wide variety of powers belong to the jurisdiction of the Soviet Union. To mention a few:

a. Representation of the USSR in international relations, conclusion, ratification and denunciation of treaties of the USSR with other states, establishment of general procedures governing the

> relations of the Union Republics with foreign states; b. Questions of war and peace; . . . d. Control over observance of the Constitution of the USSR, and insuring conformity of the Constitutions of the Union Republics with the Constitution of the USSR; e. Confirmation of alterations of boundaries between Union Republics; . . . g. Organization of the defense of the USSR, determination of directing principles governing the organization of the military formations of the Union Republics; h. Foreign trade on the basis of state monopoly; . . . k. Approval of the consolidated state budget of the USSR and of the report on its fulfillment; determination of taxes and revenues which go to the Union, Republican and local budgets.

Notwithstanding these limitations imposed on the Ukrainian SSR by Article 14 of the All-Union Constitution, the various provisions of its Ukrainian counterpart show definite signs of sovereignty and independence. Its own Article 14 speaks about the right of secession of the Ukrainian Republic from the Soviet Union. Article 15 states that the republic's territory may not be altered without its consent. Articles 15a and 15b point out, respectively, that Ukraine "has its own military formations" as well as "the right to enter into direct relations with foreign states, conclude agreements and exchange representatives with them." In Article 17 it states that "every citizen of the Ukrainian SSR is a citizen of the USSR. The citizens of all other Union Republics enjoy on the territory of the Ukrainian SSR all the rights of citizens of the Ukrainian SSR." The jurisdiction of the republic is enumerated in Article 19 which declares that "its highest organ of state power and organs of state administration" are charged with "a. Establishment of the Constitution of the Ukrainian Soviet Socialist Republic and control over its observance; . . . w. Conferring the rights of citizenship of the Ukrainian SSR; . . . z. Establishment of the manner of organizing the military formations of the Ukrainian SSR; zl. Establishment of the representation of the Ukrainian SSR in international relations." Article 43 stipulates that the Council of Ministers of Ukraine "directs the organization of the military formations of the Ukrainian SSR" (43g) and "exercises direction in the sphere of relations of the Ukrainian SSR with foreign states, following the generally established procedure by the USSR in mutual relations of the Union Republics with foreign states" (43h). Somewhat intricate and lengthy, but important, is Article 50 which asserts that

> the Ministers of the Ukrainian SSR issue within the competence of appropriate Ministries orders and instructions on the basis and in pursuance of the acting laws of the USSR and the Ukrainian SSR,

> of the decisions and directions of the Council of Ministers of the USSR and the Council of Ministers of the Ukrainian SSR, of the orders and instructions of the Union-Republican Ministries of the USSR, and verify their execution.

The right to secede from the Soviet Union (Article 17 of the USSR Constitution) strongly suggests the voluntary nature of the Soviet multinational state. Soviet writers have maintained that this right cannot be abrogated or changed or limited by the Soviet Union.(7) The right to withdraw from the USSR "means that for each union republic a practical possibility is created to freely express its will about the form of its statehood, and the will of the people within the Soviet Federation constitutes the basis of sovereignty of nations."(8) Applying the constitutional criterion only, the right of secession contained in the Soviet and the Ukrainian Constitutions looks quite impressive, indeed, and greatly enhances the argument in favor of Ukrainian independence and sovereignty.(9)

However, when the section of the Criminal Code of the Ukrainian SSR, under the heading "Crimes against the State," is examined, the value of the secession clause takes on a different meaning. In fact, Article 56 of this section, entitled "Treason to the Fatherland," unequivocally states that a citizen of the USSR is faced with severe punishment if he acts against "the territorial inviolability" of the Soviet Union.(10) An identical declaration is made by "The Law of the USSR concerning Penal Responsibility for the Crimes against the State" (Article 1).(11) In a textbook on Soviet criminal law it is explained that "the object of treason to the fatherland" is, among other things, "the inviolability" of Soviet territory.(12) One must conclude, then, that while the constitutions of the Ukrainian Republic and the Soviet Union permit Ukraine to withdraw from the Soviet "federation," Soviet criminal law, operating throughout the USSR (including Ukraine), prohibits under severe penalties even the advocacy of any such undertaking. Thus the right of secession is effectively nullified.

The constitutional provision that explicitly denies to the Soviet Union jurisdiction over the alteration of the territory of the Ukrainian SSR without its consent seems to be a strong legal safeguard of Ukrainian independence and sovereignty. Taranov explained:

> Territory is one of the integral features of the nation that formed the union republic, and together with this, the material basis of its independence. Hence it follows that the territory of any union republic may not be changed without its consent. The Union's jurisdiction as regards the territory of the union republics amounts

> only to confirmation of the decision of the union republics' organs about the border changes among them.(13)

His last sentence is obviously referring to Article 14e of the All-Union Constitution, and it should be pointed out that such a provision limits the right of Ukraine with regard to its own territorial changes. As one jurist has written, "The territory of the republics may not be changed without their consent, but it also may not be changed without the consent of the USSR, for the confirmation of the border changes among the republics belongs to the USSR. . . ."(14)

The proviso in the Ukrainian Constitution which asserts the existence of "Republican military formations"(15) is a clear and powerful manifestation of Ukrainian independence and sovereignty. Yet the paragraphs of Articles 19 and 43 mentioned previously which deal with military affairs (organization of Ukrainian military formations), besides being vague, are the only ones in the constitution that concern themselves with the armed forces of Ukraine. The Ukrainian Constitution is silent on such important matters, as, for example, institution of military ranks, appointment and removal of the high command of its armed forces, proclamation of general or partial mobilization — matters that belong to the jurisdiction of the Supreme Soviet of the USSR, specified in Article 49 of its constitution. It must be emphasized that since it is the Soviet Union which determines "directing principles governing the organization of military formations of the Union Republics," and since it also "directs the general organization of the Armed Forces of the country" (part of Article 68e), the clauses in the Ukrainian Constitution concerning the organization of military formations of the republic do not amount to anything more than a declaration of powers subordinated to USSR jurisdiction. Since, again, the question of war is outside the constitutional rights of the Ukrainian SSR, it is hard to conceive of any independent action on the part of the republic's military forces.

There is revealing statement in Article 112 of the Ukrainian Constitution: "Universal military service is the law. Military service in the ranks of the Armed Forces of the USSR is an honorable duty of the citizens of the Ukrainian SSR." This provision makes no reference to the armed forces of Ukraine but only to the forces of the Soviet Union, as if the former, contrary to Article 15a, did not exist. The logic of this significant omission becomes clearer when one reads part of Article 68e of the Soviet Union Constitution which stipulates that the All-Union Council of Ministers "fixes the annual contingent of citizens to be called up for military service. . . ." Since, according to Article 67 of the Soviet

Union Constitution, "decisions and orders of the Council of Ministers of the USSR are binding throughout the territory of the USSR,"(16) and since no provision corresponding to that part of Article 68e is to be found in the Ukrainian Constitution it is clear that, juridically speaking, only the organs of the Soviet Union are empowered to deal with the maintenance of armed forces. Upon examination, then, it must be concluded that the constitutional claim concerning Ukraine's military establishment appears to be extremely slim.(17)

One of the strongest legal arguments for regarding Ukraine as an independent and sovereign state within the limits of the "federation" is supplied by Article 15b, supported by Articles 19zl, 30j, and 30k(18) of the Ukrainian Constitution. Article 15b (Article 18a of the Soviet Union Constitution) states the right of Ukraine to be a member of the international community — that is, the right to participate directly in international discourse among states. It gives the right to separately conclude international agreements; and, finally, it allows the republic to send its diplomatic and consular representatives to foreign states as well as to receive foreign diplomatic and consular missions at home. Those are, of course, broad juridical powers suggesting strongly that Ukraine has an international legal personality. Articles 19zl, 30j, and 30k state in more specific and functional terms the competence of the Ukrainian SSR in foreign affairs, stressing the matter of Ukrainian representation abroad and foreign diplomatic representation at home. It should be noted that no specific reference is made in these articles about the competence of the Ukrainian organs of state power and administration regarding international agreements, but it may be argued that no special mention is required in light of Article 15b, which treats this important subject matter.

If only the above-mentioned constitutional provisions were taken into consideration, overlooking other clauses, or their absence, in the Ukrainian Constitution, as well as the decisive articles of the Soviet Union Constitution, then, juridically speaking, one might well assert Ukrainian independence and sovereignty in this context. Yet if all pertinent stipulations of both constitutions are considered, a different and less optimistic conclusion appears inevitable. First, Article 43h declares in unequivocal terms the subordination of the Ukrainian Council of Ministers to the USSR in the exercise of its leadership in relations with foreign states. Also, Articles 50 and 51 of the Ukrainian Constitution, which mention the subordination of the Ukrainian Ministers (including the Ministry of Foreign Affaris to the Soviet Council of Ministers and Ministries), plainly reveal the existing constitutional relationship between Ukraine and the Soviet Union in the field of international affairs.(19) This relationship is made even more vividly manifest in the provisions of the Soviet Union Constitution.

Article 14a, which assigns to the Soviet Union the "representation of the USSR in international relations," including the representation of the Ukraine as one of the constituent members of the "federation," points out the double jurisdiction of foreign affairs between the Soviet Union and the Ukrainian SSR.(20) The same article says that it is the Soviet Union which establishes the rules to be followed by the Soviet republics in their relations with foreign states, again demonstrating the supremacy of Soviet Union jurisdiction over that of the Ukrainian Republic. This article also empowers the Soviet Union to conclude, ratify, and denounce treaties of the USSR, Ukraine included, with foreign states, which, besides showing double jurisdiction in the matter of making treaties,(21) reveals two additionally important items in the Soviet Union's juridical arsenal. Reference is made here to the processes of ratification and denunciation of treaties that, according to Article 49o of the Soviet Union Constitution, are performed by the Presidium of the Supreme Soviet. No such provisions are to be found in the Ukrainian Constitution, although in practice the Ukrainian Supreme Council has exercised the right of ratification.(22) Constitutionally, however, the lack of ratification and denunciation powers limits the competence of the Ukrainian Republic with respect to international treaties.

The questions of war and peace (Article 14b of the Soviet Union Constitution), certainly very important prerogatives of any sovereign and independent state, belong to the exclusive jurisdiction of the USSR. Article 49m of the Constitution stipulates that, "in the intervals between sessions of the Supreme Soviet of the USSR," its Presidium "proclaims a state of war in the event of military attack on the USSR, or when necessary to fulfill international treaty obligations concerning mutual defense against aggression." In discussing Ukraine's lack of constitutional powers to deal with the problem of war and peace, Academician Koretskyi wrote

> The Constitution of the Ukrainian SSR does not mention the right of the Ukrainian SSR to declare war. The Constitution of the USSR ascribes to the jurisdiction of the USSR the questions of war and peace. . . . This follows from the basic aims of the voluntary union of equal Soviet Socialist Republics created for mutual aid, including defense (Article 13 of the Constitution of the USSR and the Ukrainian SSR).
>
> An attack on one of the Republics would mean an attack on the entire Soviet Union. The Ukrainian SSR, together with the Soviet

> Union, participated in the Great Patriotic War, 1941-1945, and in the conclusion of peace treaties. But the Ukrainian SSR (as well as other Union Republics) cannot separately solve questions of war and peace. Only in the solidarity and unity of all Union Republics lies the guarantee of security, integrity and sovereignty of each Union Republic and the Soviet Union.(23)

This reasoning notwithstanding, legally the sovereignty and independence of the Ukrainian Republic are sharply reduced by the simple fact that its constitution is deficient in matters of war and peace.(24)

The jurisdiction of the Ukrainian SSR, as specified by Article 19w of its constitution, contains the right to confer citizenship of the Ukrainian Republic. This right appears to be still another juridical guarantee of Ukrainian sovereignty. Since Article 17 of the Ukrainian Constitution refers to citizens of Ukraine as also being citizens of the USSR, bestowal of citizenship by Ukraine would mean not only citizenship of the Ukrainian SSR, but also of the entire Soviet Union. Conferring of citizenship on Ukrainian territory is done by the Presidium of the Supreme Council of the Ukrainian Republic, authorized in Article 3 by the law of August 19, 1938.(25) The same article also declares that is is the Presidium of the Supreme Soviet that extends citizenship of the USSR, including, of course, Soviet Union citizenship on the territory of the Ukrainian SSR, which makes it plain that there are two agencies on this territory able to impart the right of citizenship.(26) Such a state of affairs limits the jurisdiction of Ukraine concerning the right to extend citizenship, but this restriction is not the only one. According to Article 4 of the Citizenship Law of 1938, only the Presidium of the Supreme Soviet can terminate the right of citizenship of the USSR, apparently including citizenship of the Ukrainian SSR, for no such authorization for the Presidium of the Ukrainian Supreme Council may be found either in the law of 1938 or in the Ukrainian Constitution.(27)

The last point to be resolved in the discussion on the constitutional nature of Ukrainian sovereignty and independence regards the Ukrainian Constitution itself. According to Article 19a of this document, mentioned previously, the Ukrainian SSR establishes its own constitution and controls over its observance. Article 127 states that it is the Supreme Council of the Ukrainian Republic, and no other body, that enacts amendments to the constitution. Since the Ukrainian Constitution is the fundamental law of the land, legally determining such things as the social, political, and economic structure of the republic, it is of the greatest importance to know whether this basic law of the Ukraine is juridically independent of the basic law of the USSR. "The Union Republic," Zlatopol'skii maintained, "adopts its own

Constitution independently, and also independently makes in it necessary supplements and amendments, which, as also the whole Constitution itself, must conform to the Basic Law of the USSR.''(28) The logic of this revealing statement follows the provisions of both the Ukrainian and the USSR Constitutions. Having already examined the pertinent clauses of the former, mention should be made of the latter. Two articles are important here: Article 14d (quoted above) and Article 16, which reads, ''Each Union Republic has its own Constitution, which takes account of the specific features of the Republic and is drawn up in full conformity with the Constitution of the USSR.'' It is instructive that the Ukrainian Constitution is entirely silent on the matter of its ''full conformity'' with the fundamental law of the Soviet ''federation,'' but the illusion of independent jurisdiction of the Ukrainian Republic in regard to its own basic law is easily dispelled by reading the Soviet counterpart. How can anyone do anything independently if one must move within prescribed areas of activity? In short, there is a strict legal limitation imposed on the powers of the Ukrainian SSR to adopt and change its own basic law, and since this law, as the name implies, serves as the juridical groundwork for the whole state system of the Ukrainian Republic, the conditions under which it operates singularly restrict the formal exercise of Ukrainian sovereignty and independence in general.(29)

Having discussed the status of the Ukrainian Republic from the standpoint of Soviet internal law, the next step is to determine its position in the light of the law of nations. Two closely related questions must be answered: first, whether the Ukrainian SSR is a subject of international law, and second, what legal significance — if any — is to be attached to the presence of this Soviet Union Republic among the member states in the United Nations?

Generally speaking, international legal personalities are considered to be states(30) — meaning sovereign states. But, as has been shown above, Ukraine is only partially sovereign. Can such a state, then, be qualified as a subject of the law of nations? In order to answer this, one must decide (assuming that the USSR constitutes a certain form of federal state) whether a member of any federation can be regarded as a subject of international law. Prof. Korowicz wrote that ''it is generally accepted that a Member-State of a federal State, whatever may be its internal organization and autonomy, has no international personality, being represented in international relations by the central government of the federal state.''(31) He also pointed out that

> in contradistinction to the confederation of States which is a subject of international law as also, all the States belonging to the

> confederation, the federal State, and not its component parts (called States or provinces etc.), is the exclusive subject of international law. A component part of a federal State is not a State from the point of view of international law, and this is explicitly or implicitly provided in constitutions of federal States.(32)

Many international jurists would take exception to such a view by arguing that the member states of a federation have a limited international personality and therefore may be regarded as partial subjects of international law. Patrick Ransome wrote that

> states members of a federation for many purposes enjoy the rights and fulfill the duties of international Persons. They are, in the words of Professor Oppenheim, "part sovereign states and they are, consequently, International Persons for some purposes only." What these purposes are depends on the division of powers that exist in the particular federation.

He illustrated the last point by citing Switzerland as a federal state in which "member states are free to conclude treaties not only between themselves, but also with foreign states in certain specified matters." He also mentioned the United States as an example of a federation whose members are not international personalities, since the federal government alone exercises control over foreign affairs.(33)

Thus the field of external relations seems to be decisive in determining whether a member of a federation can be considered as a subject of international law. "It will therefore be seen," Ransome stated, "that, while the provisions of International Law are normally binding on fully sovereign states only, they also regulate the actions of states members of a federation in so far as those states retain control over relations with foreign states."(34) Von Schuschnigg noted that, "in contrast to sovereign States, which are the perfect subjects of International Law, States that are not fully sovereign, that is dependent States, are the imperfect or partial subjects of International Law. They are the protectorates, mandates, trusteeship territories, and the member States of a federal Union."(35) Wesley L. Gould maintained that in a federal state "the assignment of powers in international relations, hence of international personality, is a matter of constitutional law." Although he wrote that foreign affairs are usually the domain of the federal government, he nevertheless believed that examples can be found which would show that members of a federation retain "a degree of international personality."(36)

Two important factors emerge from the discussion thus far: (1) in some federations members may be considered as being partial subjects of international law — that is, they possess an international jural personality to a limited degree only; and (2) such a status is derived from the constitutional arrangement within a federal state. The latter factor is reaffirmed by Gould who said that "in respect to both confederations and federations international law generally does not undertake to assign degrees of personality to the union and its members. It accepts the arrangements made by the members."(37)

Thus, one accepts the view that the members of at least some federations — or the members of composite states resembling federations — are to be recognized as having a degree of international personality and that it is the constitutional law of a particular federation which decides whether its members are to be subjects of international law. It can safely be concluded that the Ukrainian SSR is some sort of a restricted international person or is a partial subject of the law of nations. The reason for this is obvious — both the Soviet Union and Ukrainian Constitutions assert the right of Ukraine to have relations with foreign states, thus making it a subject of international law.(38) To be sure, Soviet scholars would like us to think that the Ukrainian Republic, like any other Soviet Union Republic, is a full subject of the law of nations, as, for example, L.A. Modzhorian, who wrote that, "after giving to the Union Republics the rights of foreign relations they are, side by side with the Union, the sovereign subjects of international law."(39) Such a view is based on the assertion that the Soviet republics are sovereign states, in spite of the fact that the Soviet Union Constitution explicitly stipulates the limitation of their sovereignty by Article 14. As has been amply established with respect to the Ukrainian SSR (and thus to all the Soviet republics), however, this assertion is spurious.

Part I of this study demonstrated how the Ukrainian SSR and Belorussian SSR became members of the United Nations not so much by legal as by political means. As Gould put it, "the Ukrainian SSR and the Byelorussian SSR were admitted as original members of the United Nations as a concession to a Soviet political demand."(40) This fact notwithstanding, the legal or constitutional argument showing that these republics were capable of having direct relations with foreign countries and therefore were to be considered as states and subjects of international law, was not only useful, but, perhaps, made the difference between the acceptance or rejection of the communist request. In other words, the juridical argument had to be invoked to make the political transaction look legitimate. Once that was accomplished, then, the presence of these two Soviet Republics in the UN assumed a legal significance in its own right.

The juridical position of Ukraine in the United Nations is quite strong and is based primarily on the provisions of its Charter. Article 3 of the UN Charter affirms that the founding members of the world organization "shall be states," and Article 4, Paragraph 1, says that "membership in the United Nations is open to all peace-loving states which accept the obligations contained in the present Charter and, in the judgement of the Organization, are able and willing to carry out these obligations."(41) Article 2, Paragraph 1, declares that "the Organization is based on the principle of the sovereign equality of all its Members," and Paragraph 4 of the same article stipulates that "all Members shall refrain in their international relations from the threat of use of force against the territorial integrity or political independence of any state," thus implying that all members of the UN have a capacity to wage war. Since these measures apply to the Ukrainian SSR, the juristic status of this Soviet republic is simply this: Ukraine is a sovereign state, equal to other members, which in turn means that it has an international legal personality and is a subject of the law of nations(42); this in spite of the fact that the Ukrainian Republic is a member of a "federation." Wrestling with the same problem, Verdross wrote,

> Es kann daher kein Zweifel darüber bestehen, dass ein Gliedstaat, der als Mitlied der Vereinten Nationen aufgenommen wurde, auch ein *eigenes Völkerrechtssubject* darstellt. Diese Stellung, nimmt er aber nur gegenüber *dritten* Staaten ein, wahrend seine Stellung *innerhalb* seines Gesamtstaates ausschliesslich nach der Verfassung *dieses* Staates zu beurteilen ist. (Italics in the original.)

Noting that in the past the internation subjectivity of the members of a federation (Bundesstaat) played an insignificant role, the Austrian scholar said

> Ganz anders, steht es aber im Falle der völkerrechts-subjektivität der Ukraine und Weissrusslands, da diese im Rahmen der Charta der Vereinten Nationen den anderen Staaten gegenüber vollkommen gleichberechtigt sind und daher alle Rechte ausüben können, die den Mitgliedern der UNO zustehen.(43)

It appears, then, that the legal status of the Ukrainian SSR is much stronger in the forum of the United Nations than within the Soviet "federation"; the UN Charter is much more generous than either the Ukrainian or Soviet Union Constitutions toward Ukraine, making it a full-fledged member of the international community. As the Belgian jurist P. De Visscher put it, "Sur le plan de l'ONU la situation de l'Ukraine parait juridiquement tres forte puisque sa presence au sein de l'organisation n'est en rien liee a la presence de l'U.R.S.S. ou a la forme de son gouvernement.''(44) Such a juridical paradox makes the Ukrainian SSR at the same time both a partial and a full subject of international law, but it should not be overlooked that it is only in the United Nations organization, and nowhere else,(45) that Ukraine is invested with this distinctly normal international legal personality.(46)

Finally, it should be pointed out that there exists an enormous difference between the juristic and the political status of Ukraine, between legality and political reality. Although the latter does not constitute a subject matter of our inquiry, it would not be hard to prove that the real power in this republic resides in the communist party of the Soviet Union, of which the Ukrainian party is merely a branch.(47)

Footnotes

(1) Alexander Dallin, *The Soviet Union at the United Nations: An Inquiry into Soviet Methods and Objectives*(New York: Praeger, 1962), p. 107.

The terms ''sovereignty'' and ''independence,'' although sometimes used interchangeably, do not have the same meaning. According to one writer, ''sovereignty of a State is its supreme power over its territory and inhabitants, as well as its independence of any external authority'' (Marek St. Korowicz, *Introduction to International Law: Present Conceptions of International Law in Theory and Practice* (The Hague, Martinus Nijhoff, 1959), p. 23) He also wrote that ''independence does not mean sovereignty, it implies sovereignty. . . . It is a negative concept: the State is independent of any other state, and may not receive orders from anyone. Sovereignty . . . is a positive concept expressing the idea of what the State is authorized to do, and of what is its legal competence'' (*ibid.*, 83). Both ''sovereignty'' and ''independence'' may have either legal or political connotations; that is, there is legal and political sovereignty as well as legal and political independence. Both sovereignty and independence may be limited or reduced; there are states not fully or only partially sovereign, not fully or only partially independent.

What is the Soviet conception of sovereignty? According to Vyshinskii, ''sovereignty means the supremacy of state authority, by virtue of which that authority appears unlimited and autonomous within the land and independent in foreign relationships'' (Andrei Y. Vyshinskii, ed., *The Law of the Soviet State,* trans. from the Russian by Hugh W. Babb (with) introduction by John N. Hazard (New York: Macmillan, 1948), pp. 275-276). Prof. Levin followed Vyshinskii by defining sovereignty as ''the supremacy of state authority inside the country and its independence from whatever other authority in international relations'' (D.B. Levin, *Osnovnye problemy sovremennogo mezhdunarodnogo prava,* ed. by D. A. Haidukova (Moscow: Gosudarstvennoe izdatel'stvo iuridicheskoi literatury, 1958), p. 200). It would seem that the definition given by Korowicz does not differ substantially (in words, at least, from one presented by the Soviet writers.

(2) By the word "state" is meant "a people permanently occupying a fixed territory, bound together by common laws and customs into a body politic, possessing an organized government, and capable of conducting relations with other states.. . . States, generally speaking, may be broadly classified as sovereign or independent states and as dependent or semi-sovereign states" (Green Haywood Hackworth, *Digest of International Law,* Vol. I (Washington: U.S. Government Printing Office, 1949), p. 47). Charles Cheney Hyde, dealing with the problem of the capability of a state to have relations with other states, wrote that "there must be an assertion of right through governmental agencies to enter into relations with the outside world. The exercise of this right need not be free from external restraint. Independence is not essential. It is the possession and use of the right to enter into foreign relations, whether with or without restriction, which distinguishes States of international law from the larger number of political entities given that name and which are wholly lacking in such a privilege" (Charles Cheney Hyde, quoted in Hackworth, 47-48). "State," like "sovereignty," has both legal and political connotations.

(3) Article 13 of both Soviet Union and Ukrainian Constitutions speaks of the USSR as a Union state. The word "federal" is used only in reference to the Russian Republic (same article).

What is a federation? Comparing federation with confederation, one Soviet scholar noted that "in a federation there are several states united in one new state. . . . In a confederation two or several states, although united with one another, do not form one new state. In short, *a federation is a Union State,* while *a confederation is a Union of states* "(italics in the original) (D. L. Zlatopol'skii, *Gosudarstvennoe ustroistvo SSR* (Moscow: Gosudarstvennoe izdatel'stvo iuridicheskoi literatury, 1960), p. 6).

What is a Soviet federation? Speaking about "the political form of the state organization of the USSR," Vyshinskii stated that "the Soviet Union State is a federative state. Both by its class essence and by its organizational structure it is sharply distinguished from all existing forms of federation, confederation, and unitarianism formerly or now existing in the capitalist world. It is a type of state without a precedent in history. It emerged from the problems of the worker class dictatorship in a multi-national country. It is the realization and expression of the general will and mutual confidence of the toilers of nations with equal rights. The nationality principle at the basis of the creation of the Soviet Union State is the distinctive characteristic of the Soviet type federation" (Vyshinskii, 228-229).

Edward Mousley, a Western jurist, defined federalism as "that principle of union of political societies called states whereby the central or federal government operates for particular purposes directly on the subjects of the component states and not indirectly on them through the medium of the states united in the Federal Union, the authority of such states, each over its citizens, being confined to all remaining matters" (Edward Mousley, "The Meaning of Federalism," *Federal Union,* ed. M. Chaning-Pearce (London: Jonathan Cape, 1940), p. 21). Some Western scholars have expressed doubt about the Soviet Union being a truly federal state. Prof. Hazard wrote that "the Soviet federation has some special characteristics. It is not as loose a federation as that of the United States, and by no means as decentralized as Canada or Australia" (John N. Hazard, *The Soviet System of Government,* rev. ed (Chicago: University of Chicago Press, 1960), p. 76). The author felt that the powers of the Soviet republics within the federation are quite limited. (*ibid.,* 87-88). Wheare regarded the Soviet state as quasi-federal; he was of the opinion that "if the full powers conferred by Article 14 of the Constitution upon the All-Union Government are exercised in practice — and there seems every reason why they should be — very little of the federal principle remains in the government of the USSR" (K. C. Wheare, *Federal Government,* 3rd ed. (London: Oxford University Press, 1953), pp. 26-28). Prof. Korowicz wrote that the USSR "is a federal state of a special type, because it has many legal features of a confederation of States, and even more features of a *highly centralized State.. . .* The USSR is neither a confederation nor a federation; it is virtually a unitary State (italics in the original) (Korowicz, 279-280). Towster, whose opinion in part is similar to Korowicz's, claimed that "in its federal features the U.S.S.R. resembles more the United States than the British commonwealth, but by written constitution or unwritten attitude it has also some confederative and strongly unitary characteristics. The nationality aspect of Soviet federal arrangements, which distinguishes the U.S.S.R. from all other federal states, constitutes a unique contribution to political theory and practice" (Julian Towster, *Political Power in the U.S.S.R. 1917-1947: The Theory and and Structure of Government in the Soviet State* (New York: Oxford University Press, 1948), p. 379). It is not the purpose of this study to investigate in detail the nature of the political structure of the Soviet state and to arrive at a concrete conclusion, but for practical considerations the designation of the USSR as a Soviet-type federation or "federation" will be sufficient.

(4) Zlatopol'skii, 113.

(5) It is understood that there is no need to examine all the relevant articles in the two constitutions.

(6) The constitutional status of all other Soviet republics is the same.

(7) A. P. Taranov, *Osnovni pryncypy konstytutsii Ukrains'koi RSR* (Kiev: Vydavnytstvo Adademii Nauk Ukrain'skoi RSR, 1962), p. 105; Zlatopol'skii, 155. This assertion notwithstanding, Vyshinskii wrote that "an amendment to the draft of the Constitution of the USSR, introduced while it was being considered by the entire people, proposed to exclude Article 17 from the draft. Stalin pointed out in his report at the Extra-ordinary Eighth All-Union Congress of Soviets that this proposal was wrong and should not be adopted by the Congress" (Vyshinskii, 285). It is conceivable, therefore, that at some future date, an amendment to annual Article 17, which would abrogate the right of secession, could be proposed successfully.

(8) Taranov, 105.

(9) An attempt by Prof. Aspaturian to prove that the right of secession has no meaning even constitutionally, while interesting, falls short of the mark. According to him, Article 6 of the Soviet Union Constitution (which declares that the land in the USSR is the property of the state) contravenes the right of the republics to leave the Soviet Union. This is because, since their territory is owned by the USSR, to secede would actually mean "the willingness of the Union to abdicate its title of ownership over the land of the Republics. . . ." (Aspaturian, 127). It appears that Aspaturian did not think that the Soviet republics own or possess the territory on which they exist, a rather untenable proposition. It would be more correct to say that, constitutionally, the USSR and each of its republics (within its respective borders) own the same territory. In case any of the republics decides to withdraw from the "federation," this

double proprietorship of the land ceases; the territory becomes solely the property of the seceding republic. It should also be noted that, if one accepts the notion of the Soviet Union republics owning no territory, then, of course, one could not regard them legally as states, for territory is one of the essential elements of any state. Such a conclusion would not only be contrary to Aspaturian's judgment, but would also indicate that the Soviet constitution makers committed an elementary mistake with regard to the juridical status of the republics. They declared that they were sovereign states, yet that the territory was not actually theirs but was owned by the Soviet Union — an unlikely possibility. Then again, Article 18 of the USSR Constitution stipulates that "the territory of a Union Republic may not be altered without its consent." Had the Soviet Union been the sole proprietor of the land of the entire "federation," it would not make much sense to have such a clause in the constitution. Aspaturian quoted Vyshinskii (*The Law of the Soviet State,* 285-286) to give weight to his legal arguments, although Vyshinskii nowhere stated that the republics' territories are not owned by them. On the contrary, Vyshinskii wrote that "each Union Republic as a state has a definite state territory whose boundaries have precisely established the limit in space of the state authority of that republic and which is the basis of its economic activity" *(ibid.,* 286).

(10) *Ugolovnoe zakonodatel'stvo Soiuza SSR i soiuznykh Respublic,* Vol. I (Moscow: Gosudarstvennoe izdatel'stvo iuridicheskoi literatury, 1963), p. 188. Reference is to the Criminal Code of the Ukrainian SSR, adopted in 1960. The previous criminal code of 1927 contained the same provision — Chapter I, "Counterrevolutionary Crimes," 541a) (see *Kryminál'nyikodeks Ukrains'koi RSR* (Kiev: Derzhavne vydavnytstvo politychnoi literatury URSR, 1958), p. 19). It should be pointed out that Chapter 8 of this work, unlike the preceding chapters, is not strictly historical; that is it does not restrict its field of inquiry to the period 1944-1950. The juridical status of Ukraine will not only apply to the said period, but also to the present time. It is true that some changes occurred in Soviet constitutional and municipal law during and since the years 1944-1950, but for the purpose of this study, these changes are not important or essential, and a discussion of them is not necessary. The legal position of the Ukrainian SSR today is the same as it was in the period with which this work is concerned, and since this is so, the use, for example, of the later edition of the Ukrainian Criminal Code, whose specific contents pertaining to the matter of secession have remained unchanged, is not an anachronism.

(11) Ugolovnoe zakonodatel'stvo Soiuza SSR i soiuznykh Prespublik, Vol. I, 44.

(12) *Sovetskoe ugolovnoe pravo* (Moscow: Gosuderstvennoe izdatel'stvo iuridicheskoi literatury, 1962), p. 23.

(13) Taranov, 104.

(14) V. Lysyi, "Derzhavnyi status USSR ta inshykh soiuznykh Respublic SSSR," *Vilna Ukraina,* No. 34 (1962), p. 17.

(15) Article 18b of the All-Union Constitution says that "each Union Republic has its own Republican military formations."

(16) See also Articles 50 and 51 of the Ukrainain Constitution, which state the subordination of the Ukrainian ministries to Soviet Union ministries.

(17) It is curious that both Taranov and Zlatopol'skii wrote about the rights of the republics to have their own military formations rather than about the

existence of such formations, distinctly mentioned by the All-Union and Soviet Union Republic Constitutions. (see Taranov, 108; and Zlatopol'skii, 159, 166). In fact, Ukrainian military formations were never created.

(18) Articles 30j and 30k affirm, respectively, that the Presidium of the Supreme Council of the Ukrainian Republic ''appoints and recalls plenipotentiary representatives of the Ukrainian SSR to foreign states'' and ''receives the letters of credence and recall of the diplomatic representatives of foreign states accredited to it.''

(19) Texts on Soviet administrative law clearly state that the Ministries of Foreign Affairs of the Union Republics follow, among other things, the directions of the Ministry of Foreign Affairs of the USSR (see V. A. Vlasov and S. S. Studenikin, *Sovetskoe administrativnoe pravo* (Moscow: Gosudarstvennoe izdatel'stvo iuridicheskoi literatury, 1959), p. 223; also A. E. Lynev, ed. *Administrativnoe pravo* (Moscow: Izdatel'stvo ''Iuridicheskaia Literatura,'' 1967), p. 526).

(20) This double jurisdiction is not equal, as Article 68 d of the Soviet Union Constitution shows: ''The Council of Ministers of the USSR exercises general guidance in the sphere of relations with foreign states.'' Corresponding provisions of the Soviet Union Constitution to Articles 30j and 30k of the Ukrainian Constitution are contained in Articles 49 p and 49q.

(21) There seems to be a misunderstanding concerning the question of whether Soviet Union republics have a right to conclude treaties. Aspaturian and Lysyi believed they have no such right (Aspaturian, 161; Lysyi, 19). However, as the Soviet author Ianovskii explained, the term ''agreement'' *(soglashenie)*, which is used by the constitutions of the USSR and the Soviet Union republics (in Ukrainian, *uhoda)*, when describing the rights of the Republics *vis-a-vis* foreign states, includes in its meaning also treaties *(dogovory)*, M.N. Ianovskii, ''Sovetskie soiuznye Respubliki — polnopravnye subekty mezhdunarodnogo prava,'' *Sovetskoe gosudarstvo i pravo,* Vol. XII (1962), p. 58. As is known, the Ukrainian SSR was a party to five international peace treaties with Bulgaria, Italy, Rumania, Hungary, and Finland (see L. K. Palamarchuk, ed., *Ukrains'ka SSR u mizhnarodnikh vidnosynakh,* (Kiev: Vydavnytstvo Akademii Nauk Ukrains'koi RSR, 1959), pp. 58-168; see also N. M. Ul'ianova, ''Mizhnarodni dohovory Radians'koi Ukrainy,'' *Radians'ke pravo,* No. 11, 1966, pp. 88-92).

(22) In 1947 it ratified all five peace treaties mentioned above. In 1963 it also ratified the treaty prohibiting testing of nuclear weapons in the atmosphere, outer space, and underwater. Besides treaties, many other agreements, conventions, charters, etc., were ratified by the Ukrainian SSR (see N. M. Ul'ianova, ''Uchast' Ukrains'koi RSR u mizhnarodnich konferentsiiakh i mizhnarodnich dohovorakh,'' in *Ukrains'ka Radians'ka Sotsialistychna Respublika,* ed. M. P. Bazhan *et al.* (Kiev: Akademiia Nauk Ukrains'koi RSR, 1965), pp. 632-634). Ianovskii suggested that the constitutions of the Sovet Union republics should have provisions giving the republics the right to ratify international treaties or agreements. He also proposed that the right to denounce treaties should be included in the constitutions. (see Ianovskii, 59). A somewhat ingenious explanation regarding the absence of ratification and denunciation powers in the Ukrainian Constitution is presented by Koretskyi. He wrote, ''Although the Constitution of the Ukrainian SSR does not mention the right to conduct ratification and denunciation of treaties, this does not mean that such a right does not exist. It is logically connected with the right to conclude treaties''

(V. M. Koretskyi, "Mizhnarodno-pravna sub'ektnist' Ukrain'skoi RSR," in *Ukrains'ka Radians'ka Sotsialistychna Respublika,* (Kiev: Akademiia Nauk Ukrains'koi RSR, 1965), p. 628).

(23) *Ibid.,*

(24) The sovereignty of Ukraine is again reduced by the exclusive jurisdiction of the Soviet Union over foreign trade (Article 14h of the Soviet Union Constitution).

(25) This law is entitled "Citizenship of the Union of Soviet Socialist Republics," and was passed by the Supreme Soviet of the USSR (*Sbornik zakonov SSSR i ukazov Presidiuma Verkhovnogo Soveta SSSR (1938-July 1956)*(Moscow: Gosudarstvennoe izdatel'stvo iuridicheskoi literatury, 1956), p. 64). Article 30g of the Ukrainian Constitution mentions the power of the Presidium of the Supreme Council of the Ukrainian SSR to bestow its citizenship.

(26) It is obvious that a foreigner who was given Soviet Union citizenship on the territory of Ukraine by the Presidium of the Supreme Soviet of the USSR automatically becomes a citizen of the Ukrainian Republic.

(27) It may be argued that there is still another limitation of Ukrainian juridical sovereignty and independence here. Article 17 of the Ukrainian Constitution additionally stipulates that citizens of all other Soviet republics have the rights of Ukrainian SSR citizens when they are on its territory, which simply means that they become citizens of Ukraine, just by crossing its borders. A foreigner, for example, who was granted citizenship by the Presidium of the Supreme Soviet of the Georgian SSR, by entering Ukraine, becomes its citizen by this very act, without any action on the part of Ukrainian authorities.

(28) Zlatopol'skii, 163.

(29) It is, of course, possible to cite still other articles of both the Ukrainian and Soviet Union Constitutions to show the juridical limitations of Ukrainian sovereignty, but enough was said to warrant a definite conclusion.

The argument of Soviet writers (see Taranov, 109; Ianovskii, 56) that the sovereignty of Ukraine, or of the Soviet Union republics in general, is constitutionally exercised — and therefore apparently enhanced — by the fact that they are represented in the All-Union organs of government as, for example, in the Soviet of Nationalities (Article 35 of the Soviet Union Constitution) does not, in my opinion, in any way, change the existing constitutional set-up in the Soviet "federal" state. The legal restrictions of Ukrainian sovereignty and independence remain untouched by the participation of the representative of the Ukrainian SSR in the Soviet government organs.

(30) "The classicial doctrine of International Law generally regarded only civilized, sovereign States as international persons and therefore as subjects of International Law. The Law of Nations was defined as the body of rules governing independent States in their relations with one another" (Kurt von Schuschnigg, *International Law: An Introduction to the Law of Peace* (Milwaukee: Bruce Publishing Company, 1959), p. 69). "International law is generally defined or described as being applicable to relations between states. States are said to be the subjects of international law . . ." Philip C. Jessup, *A Modern Law of Nations: An Introduction* (New York: Macmillan, 1948), p. 15. Besides states, also individuals, international organizations, etc., are considered by many Western jurists as having an international personality. Soviet writers, as a rule, maintain that only states (sovereign states) and nations

fighting for their independence are subjects of international law. See, for example, F. I. Kozhevnikov, ed. *Mezhdunarodnoe pravo* (Moscow: Gosudarstvennoe izdatel'stvo iuridicheskoi literatury, 1957), pp. 86-87; L. A. Modzhorian, *Sub'ekty mezhdunarodnogo prava* (Moscow: Gosudarstvennoe izdatel'stvo iuridicheskoi literatury, 1958).

(31) Korowicz, 82.

(32) *Ibid.*, 277. It must be said that the USSR Constitution neither explicitly nor implicitly refers to the members of the Soviet Union (claimed by the Soviets to be a federation) as not being states under international law.

Korowicz of course, is not the only scholar who thought that members of the federation cannot be treated as subjects of the law of nations. Dolan, dealing with the matter of our concern, was of the same opinion. He relied on Josef Kunz's judgment (J.L. Kunz, *Die Staatenverbindungen* (Stuttgart: Verlog von W. Kohlhammer, 1929), p. 664 that "only federations and not their members are subjects of International law, . . ." (see Edward Dolan, "The Member Republics of the U.S.S.R. as Subjects of the Law of Nations," *The International and Comparative Law Quarterly,* Vol. IV (1955), p. 633).

(33) Patrick Ransome, "Federation and International Law," in *Federal Union,* 240.

(34) *Ibid.*

(35 Von Schuschnigg, 72.

(36) Wesley L. Gould, *An Introduction to International Law* (New York: Harper Brothers, 1957), p. 200.

(37) *Ibid.*, 200-201.

(38) Discussing the heart of the problem, Prof. Halaichuk wrote: "If a member of a federation is to be subject in international law, it is necessary for the member to have the proper power recognized by the federal constitution. Is a constitutional provision alone sufficient? . . . Soviet authors believe that a constitutional provision suffices. S. Krylov stated: 'The law (of February 1, 1944) clearly confirms that the Soviet Republics are subjects of international law.' The matter was even more clearly stated by Tunkin. In the course of the U.N. International Law Commission's work on the codification of diplomatic law, the Austrian scholar A. von Verdross raised the question whether mention should be made of members of federations who enjoyed the right of legation. Tunkin answered: 'As stated by Mr. Verdross, the question whether a member-state of a federation has the right of legation depends on the federal constitution and is not a question of international law' " (see Bohdan T. Halaichuk, "The Soviet Ukraine as a Subject of International Law," in *The Annals of the Ukrainian Academy of Arts and Sciences in the United States,* Vol. IX (1961), pp. 170-171).

Koretskyi maintained, interestingly enough, that the Ukrainian SSR retained its international legal subjectivity *(sub'ektnist')* even after joining the USSR and transferring the conduct of its foreign relations to the Union. This would mean, of course, that Ukraine was a subject of international law before the constitutional changes of 1944. The noted Ukrainian jurist seemingly explained this legal *tourde force* by stating that the Ukrainian Republic, as well as other Soviet republics, had the right to take part in Soviet Union organs of external relations (and thus apparently to participate in foreign affairs)(see Koretskyi, in *Ukrains'ka Radians'ka Sotsialistychna Respublika,* 627). Brovka believed, waging a slight polemic against many of his Soviet colleagues, that it was a mistake to attribute international legal subjectivity *(pravosub'eknost')*to the Union republics merely on the strength of the USSR law of February 1944. Basing his conclusion on the decisive importance of sovereignty, he declared that "the Soviet Republics arose as independent sovereign states. They preserved their sovereignty even after entering the USSR. Therefore, their international subjectivity was not interrupted in the course of their development. With the adoption of the law of February 1, 1944, it received still clearer expression" (see Brovka, *Mezhdunarodnaia pravosub'ektnost BSSR,* 83-84). It is possible to admire the legal ingenuity of the Soviet writers without agreeing with them.

(39) Modzhorian, 64. Brovka wrote that "the USSR and the Union Republics manifest themselves on the international arena independently and are full subjects of international law" (Brovka, 89). As the title of Ianovskii's article indicates, its author regarded the Soviet republics as full subjects of the law of nations (see Ianovskii, 55).

(40) Gould, 201.

(42) Article 34 (1) of the Statute of the International Court of Justice provides that "only states may be parties in cases before the Court." The statute is part of the UN Charter, and the International Court of Justice is the principal judicial organ of the UN. All the UN members are *ipso facto* parties to the statute.

(42) Perhaps it would be of some interest to cite the legal opinion of several Western scholars concerning the presence of Ukraine (and Belorussia) in the United Nations. Goodrich wrote that "the principle that states alone would be members of the Organization was never applied in any narrow sense. In fact it would be difficult to justify the inclusion of Ukraine and Byelorussia under any generally accepted definition of a state in international law" (Leland M. Goodrich, *The United Nations*(New York: Thomas Y. Crowell, 1959), p. 86). Dealing with the Stalin constitution and the presence of the Ukrainian and Belorussian Republics in the international organization, von Schuschnigg asserted that "the constitutional language and the separate UN membership of two Russian member States are, from a legal point of view, manifestly irrelevant; they constitute one of those anomalies which demonstrates the frequent incongruence of juristic theory and political practice" (von Schuschnigg, 77). Having in mind Ukraine and Belorussia, Gould noted that "an anomaly is introduced when an entity lacking the status of a state is admitted as a member of an international organization of states"; he further stated that "whatever the degree of international personality that may be derived from membership in the United Nations, the Ukrainian and Byelo-Russian Republics are not states." (Gould, 201).

All these statements, true or false, in no way affect the stipulations of the Charter, which, if anything else, should be binding.

(43) Alfred Verdross, "Die Volkerrechtssubjektivitat der Gliedstaaten der Sowjetunion," *Osterreichische Zeitschrift fur Offentliches, Recht,* Vol. I (1946), p. 218. See also Romain Yakemtchouk, *L'Ukraine en Droit International* (Louvain: Centre Ukraïnien d'Etudes en Belgique, 1954), pp. 43-44.

(44) Paul De Visscher, "A propos de la personnalite juridique de l'Ukraine," *L'Ukraine dans le cadre de l'Est Europeen* (Louvain: Editions Nauwelaerts, 1957), pp. 104-105.

(45) It may be argued, as Yakemtchouk did, that the diplomatic activity of the Ukrainian SSR in the international forum outside the UN — for example,

participation in the Paris Conference of 1946, signing the peace treaties in 1947, etc. — indicates yet another area in which Ukraine appears to be a full subject of international law. However, one cannot see why a limited international personality (a deficient state only partially sovereign) under certain circumstances should not be engaged in these acts. See Yakemtchouk, 42-43. See also Yakemtchouk, 36-37; *Ukrains'ka SSR u mizhnarodnikh vidnosynakh,* 11; and Yaroslav Bilinskyi, *The Second Soviet Republic: The Ukraine after World War II*(New Brunswick: Rutgers University Press, 1964), pp. 266-267, for a brief discussion of Ukrainian diplomatic involvement outside the UN.

(46) An interesting question which presents itself in connection with the membership of Ukraine in the UN is, whether this country was given recognition by other members of the international organization. Halaichuk maintained — concentrating his attention on the United States — that since Washington agreed to the UN membership of Ukraine and Belorussia, it definitely recognized them: "The rule of international law permits no doubt that the United States have recognized Ukraine and Byelorussia *de jure.*" Halaichuk built his case on the opinion of many jurists (see Bohdan Halaichuk, "Has the United States Recognized Ukraine," in *The Ukrainian Quarterly,* Vol. XI (1955), pp. 24-28). However, the United States government had an opposite view on this matter. An official publication of the U.S. Department of State declared that "Although Belorussia . . . and Ukraine . . . have status as members of the United Nations, they are regarded by the US Government only as constituent parts of the Soviet Union"; this publication further stated that "the US Government does not recognize Belorussia and Ukraine as independent states, . . ." (U.S. Department of State, Bureau of Intelligence and Research, *Status of the World's Nations* (Geographic Bulletin No. 2) (Washington: U.S. Government Printing Office, 1967), pp. 8, 13). The entire problem of the relationship between recognition and UN membership, or the representation of member states in the UN, received a brief exposition in a memorandum "Legal Aspects of Problem of Representation in the United Nations," prepared in 1950 for Trygve Lie, then Secretary-General of the UN. The authoritative conclusions of this memorandum, based on "the unbroken practice of the UN members, left no doubt that (1) A member could properly vote to accept a representative of a government which it did not recognize or with which it had no diplomatic relations, and (2) Such a vote did not imply recognition or a readiness to assume diplomatic relations," (Security Council, *Records,* Fifth Year, Supplement for January, February, March 1950 (Doc. S 1466), 18-23.

(47) Meyer wrote that "As sovereign of the Soviet Union, the Party (that is, its highest decision-making organization) not only determines basic policies and thus defines the goals of the entire system. It also shapes the structure within which the goals are to be attained and the policies carried out. In other words, the Party organizes and reorganizes the government, the entire administration, the entire associational life of the society; it does so in sovereign fashion, unencumbered by any fundamental respect for the institution it has itself created. This, of course, is a sharp negation of the very notion of constitutionalism. A constitution establishes rules of the game for the political process and creates certain structures which it endows with authority. In the USSR, all governmental authority is derived from the Party and the Party can take it away; the Party can also change the rules of the game" (Alfred G. Meyer, *The Soviet Political System: An Interpretation* (New York: Random

House, 1965), p. 114). On the decisive rôle of the Soviet Communist Party, see also Hazard; Fainsod; and Leonard Shapiro, *The Communist Party of the Soviet Union* (New York: Random House, 1964), and Abdurakhman Avtorkhanov, *The Communist Party Apparatus* (Celveland: World Publishing House, 1966).

CHAPTER 9
ANOTHER SOVIET DELEGATION: CONCLUSION
Moscow's Alter Ego

The Ukrainian SSR became a founding member of the United Nations through the skillful performance of Soviet diplomacy. Soon the Ukrainian delegation, ably led by Dmytro Manuilsky, began to display great interest in some of the vexing problems which immediately confronted the UN upon its founding. Victory over the Axis Powers brought almost immediate discord into the Allied camp, and the UN forum found itself on many occasions yet another battleground in the burgeoning conflict between the Western Powers and the Soviet Union. In this battle of words which expressed the widening rift between the World War II partners, an additional voice for the Krelim policies in the UN was more than welcome; the help of the Ukrainian delegation was needed.(1)

The record of the major diplomatic activities of Ukraine at the United Nations in 1946, 1948, and 1949 attests to Ukraine's active participation in various issues that beset the postwar world. The record also shows that the representatives of the Ukrainian SSR consistently supported Soviet positions, and, in fact, the policies of the Ukrainian delegation were indistinguishable from those of the USSR delegation. The Ukrainian Republic is, after all, a constituent part of the USSR, and, as has been shown in the previous chapter, its juridical status within the Soviet-type federation is not conducive to any independent action. Regarding the conduct of Ukraine's foreign relations, it cannot be overemphasized that the pertaining constitutional (and, therefore, institutional) arrangement within the Soviet Union leaves no doubt that the Ukrainian Ministry of Foreign Affairs takes its orders from the Soviet All-Union counterpart, thus placing the Ukrainian delegation under Moscow's direction. It should however be stressed that the legal position of the Ukrainian emissaries in the United Nations indicates no such dependency.

During this study of Ukraine's diplomatic performance at the UN, it was interesting to observe that on several occasions — for example, in the Czechoslovakian or AEC matters — the Ukrainian delegates appeared to be speaking not only for Ukraine, but also for the Soviet Union. On the other hand, there was no single occurrence examined herein in which USSR spokesmen also tried to represent the Ukrainian SSR. It may be rightly argued that the Soviet delegates, merely by being the representatives of the Soviet Union, are also *ipso facto*, the representatives of Ukraine, There must have been moments during the debates when Gromyko and Malik were tempted to do that; however, they never did. But why did Tarasenko, and especially Manuilsky, sometimes behave as if they represented both Ukraine and the USSR? Was it just overzealousness on their part? Or was it a conscious effort to impress on UN members and the world that in the Soviet federal state not only does the Soviet Union speak for its members, but Soviet Union republics can also speak on behalf of the USSR (thus demonstrating the superiority of the Soviet-made federation)? — It seems this latter reasoning is more plausible.

In the Soviet Union the importance of a state official, especially of high rank, is determined by his status in the Communist Party. Manuilsky (1883-1959), head of the Ukrainian delegation to the UN between 1945 and 1950 as well as being the Ukrainian foreign minister between 1944 and 1952, became a candidate-member of the Central Committee of the Party as early as 1922, at the Eleventh Congress. At the next congress, in 1923, Manuilsky was elected a full member of the Central Committee, and from that time on, he was successively reelected through the Eighteenth Congress, in 1939. (The Nineteenth Congress took place only in 1952). In the Ukrainian branch of the Communist Party he twice served on the Politburo — from 1920 to 1923 and again from 1949 to 1952.

Andrei Gromyko (born in 1909), head of the USSR delegation from 1946 to 1948, was elected a candidate of the Central Committee at the Nineteenth Congress and became a full member at the Twentieth Congress in 1956; in April 1973 he became a member of the Politburo. Malik (born in 1906), head of the Soviet delegation from 1948 to 1952, does not appear to have been either a candidate-member or a full member of the Central Committee.(3) Since it is obvious that the three Soviet delegations met together to plan actions and to devise strategies and tactics (although no available documentary evidence exists for this), an important and somewhat intriguing question arises concerning the role played by Manuilsky in the company of Gromyko or Malik. Who presided over the meetings — the chief USSR representative or the chief Ukrainian delegate? Even more significant, who was actually in charge of the entire Soviet mission to the United Nations (comprising all three delegations) when the UN was in session?(4) And when there were problems to be resolved and decisions to make immediately, with no time to contact Moscow, which delegate exercised ultimate authority?

Although it is not known with certainty, it would be strange, indeed, if a man of Manuilsky's stature subordinated himself to people (able though they were) more than twenty years his juniors, who had never served on the prestigious Central Committee as he had done. It does not seem improbable, then, that Manuilsky, when at the UN, was actually in command of the entire Soviet contingent, while outwardly leading only the Ukrainian delegation. In closely examining the disputes in which he participated — for example, the Greek or Palestinian cases — one can almost "feel" Manuilsky's personal force in leading the charge from the Soviet camp. The respect for Manuilsky accorded by the USSR representatives seems more than just a courtesy.

When an individual of Manuilsky's achievements was appointed to head the Ukrainian delegation to the UN, perhaps it could have been anticipated that Ukraine was to play a prominent part in Moscow's designs on that forum and to make a considerable contribution to Soviet UN diplomacy.(5) A cautionary note might be sounded regarding the importance of these contributions or the Ukrainian role at the UN in general, for, as some scholars think, the Soviet Union has never regarded this international organization as a primary arena for its political actions.(6) However, within the limited range of political options available, the Ukrainian delegation made its imprint in UN affairs.

What political value did Moscow derive from the major diplomatic activities of Ukraine at the UN during this period? The main benefits appear to lie in the field of propaganda or psychological warfare, as was the case with the disputes over Indonesia, in which Ukrainian diplomats attacked the Western Powers for their policies, real or imagined, of pursuing the path of colonialism and imperialism while at the same time playing advocates of national independence. It was the same with the Czechoslovak matter, where the charge of a communist conspiracy and coup was denied and the victory of communism in Czechoslovakia was defended and justified, while Cold War enemies were blamed for interfering in the internal affairs of that country, and lessons in diplomatic history meant to discredit both Paris and London were taught. This psychological warfare also appeared during the atomic disarmament controversy, in which the United States was constantly accused of seeking to impose its will on the world through its monopoly of nuclear weapons, while the USSR was pictured as a defender of national sovereignties against the American "ruling circles." These cases, and others, left no doubt as to an intense preoccupation of the Ukrainian delegation with propaganda which, in our own age, in Hans Morgenthau's words, "has become an autonomous instrument of foreign policy, coordinated with the traditional instruments of diplomacy and military force."(7)

To be sure, it is almost impossible to ascertain the effects of these campaigns of psychological warfare waged by the Ukrainian SSR. The Soviet Union, Ukraine, and other communist countries were constantly outvoted by other members of the United Nations and their proposals defeated; the Soviet bloc constituted a minority in the UN, and, were it not for the USSR, it could have been totally ignored. The Ukrainian delegation, as part of this minority, shared all the Soviet Union's frustrations and failures. However its association with a Great Power, whether in defeat or in victory, Ukraine's status and political weight in the United Nations and elsewhere in the world could not have been entirely insignificant.

To illustrate, consider the problem of national independence versus colonialism. In the immediate postwar period, many nations, especially in Asia, strove for independence from Western colonialism; such a development presented the Kremlin leaders with an opportunity to capitalize on these Western difficulties by championing the cause of national sovereignty. In the Indonesian situation, the Ukrainian delegation was given the task of initiating the debate that became a starting point for Soviet verbal blasts against the "colonialist" and "imperialist" countries. In this dispute the Ukrainian emissaries, together with their Soviet colleagues, assumed the role of experts on the "colonial question". Beneficial to Moscow was the fact that, by allowing Ukraine to play a dominant role in exposing the "evils of colonialism," Moscow's own positive solution to the so-called "national question" could be demonstrated. Here was one of the Soviet Union's republics, a former subjugated province of Tsarist Russia, behaving in the manner of a sovereign state and speaking about the national freedom and rights of the Indonesian people. An impression was created that the national voice of this republic must be free, if it concerned itself so boldly with the national freedom of others.(8) Who could be a better authority than a nation with a record of past subjugation: a nation which, thanks to the Soviet regime, had achieved its independence? Even if the other member believed Ukraine's posturing, however, it would still be difficult to assess Soviet propaganda gains, as it would be to evaluate other matters in which the Ukrainian delegation played a significant role.

Yet it still would appear, from this study of the major diplomatic activities of Ukraine in the UN, that Stalin and his associates had every reason to be satisfied with Ukraine's performance. Manuilsky's team proved to be as skillful as was possible under admittedly unfavorable circumstances (i.e., Washington's domination of the UN). The three

Soviet delegations worked in unison, and the communist spokesmen for Ukraine became a reliable instrument of Moscow's foreign policy.

In the UN, the delegates of the Ukrainian SSR speak in the name of the Ukrainian nation and claim that they represent a sovereign independent state — a claim this research disputes. It has been demonstrated that even two Soviet constitutions (that of the Ukrainian SSR and the Soviet Union) cannot hide the manifest limitations and deficiencies of the Ukrainian Republic within the Soviet "federation." Juridically, Ukraine is not a normal state, and its sovereignty and independence fall far short of any generally accepted definitions of these terms. Yet this too is fact: Ukraine is a member of the United Nations, which, according to its Charter, must consist of sovereign and independent states. The paradox is obvious. Can it be contrary to reason, international law, and common sense to regard a nation of over forty million people as ineligible to stand among other countries in an organization of nations? "It is sometimes forgotten," Prof. Aspaturian wrote,

> that whereas the Union Republics are fictional states, for the most part they represent genuine nations. . . . Not only are Republics like the Ukraine, the Baltic countries, Georgia, Armenia and some Central Asian Republics more culturally compact and historically evolved national communities than many of the artificial nations of Latin America (and of the Arab world) or the tribal prenational communities of Africa, but they also possess more of the fundamental prerequisites for self-government, independence and national recognition.(9)

It would seem that the Ukrainian nation, a historically forged community of people, has an inherent right to belong to the world organization of a civilized society, whether it can or cannot be regarded as a sovereign independent state and whether it is represented by real or fictitious advocates.

Footnotes

(1) It should be pointed out that between 1945 and 1950 the chief support for Soviet policies in the UN, excluding Ukraine and Belorussia, came only from Poland, Czechoslovakia, and Yugoslavia. (Hungary, Rumania, Albania, and Bulgaria were not admitted until 1955.)

(2) One also cannot disregard the fact that it is the Communist Party of the Soviet Union that decides all questions of foreign policy for the entire Soviet Union, including Ukraine.

(3) On Manuilsky, see *Ukrains'ka Radians'ka Entsyklopedia,* 464-465, and *Sovetskaia Istoricheskaia Entsiklopedia* (Moscow: Izdatel'stvo Sovetskaia

Entsiklopediia, 1966), Vol. IX, p. 46. On Gromyko, see *Diplomaticheskii Slovar'* (Moscow: Gosudarstvennoe izdatel'stvo politicheskoi literatury, 1960-1964), Vol. I, p. 413-414; and *Sovetskaia Istoricheskaia Entsiklopediia,* IV,799. On Malik, see *Diplomaticheskii Slovar',* II:248; his name does not appear in *Sovetskaia Istoricheskaia Entsiklopediia.*

(4) The Ukrainian delegation did not have a permanent mission to the United Nations until 1959.

(5) After the departure of Manuilsky from the UN the "golden age" of Ukrainian Soviet diplomacy was over. This can be proved by researching Ukrainian activities and influences in the UN during the past two and one-half decades.

(6) See Dallin, *The Soviet Union at the United Nations,* 25.

(7) Hans J. Morgenthau, *Politics among Nations: The Struggle for Power and Peace,* 4th ed. (New York: Knopf, 1967), p. 324.

(8) Some observers must have been struck by the ironic situation in which the representatives of Soviet Ukraine found themselves, for they were talking about the things they lacked themselves.

(9) Aspaturian, 201.

BIBLIOGRAPHY

Documents

Documents of the United Nations Conference on International Organization, San Francisco, 1945. Vol. 1, General. London, New York, 1945.

Great Britain, 5 *Parliamentary Debates* (Commons), 408, cols. 1267-1295. London: His Majesty's Stationary Office, 1945.

Kryminal'nyi kodeks Ukrains'koi RSR (Criminal code of the Ukrainian SSR). Kiev: Derzhavne vydavnytstvo politychnoi literatury URSR, 1958.

Sovetskoe ugolovnoe pravo (Soviet criminal law). Moscow: Gosudarstvennoe izdatel'stvo iuridicheskoi literatury, 1962.

SSR. Ministerstvo Inostrannykh Del. *Perepiska Predsedatelia Soveta Ministrov SSR z Prezidentami SSHA i Prem'er-Ministrami Velikobritannii vo vremia Velikoi Otechestvennoi Voiny, 1941-1945.* (USSR. Ministry of Foreign Affairs. Correspondence between the Chairman of the Council of Ministers of the U.S.S.R., and the Presidents of the U.S.A. and the Prime Ministers of Great Britain during the Great Patriotic War of 1941-1945). 2 vols. Moscow: Gosudarstvennoe izdatel'stvo politicheskoi literatury, 1957.

Teheran, Ialta i Potsdam: Sbornik dokumentov. (Teheran, Yalta and Potsdam: Collection of documents). Moscow: Izdatel'stvo "Mezhdunarodnye otnosheniia," 1967.

Ugolovnoe zakonodatel'stvo Soiuza SSR i soiuznykh Respublik (Criminal code of the Union of Soviet Socialist republics and the Union republics). Moscow: Gosudarstvennoe izdatel'stvo iuridicheskoi literatury, 1963.

Ukrains'ka RSR. Ministerstvo Inostranykh Dil. *Ukrains'ka RSR na mizhnarodnii areni: Zbirnyk dokumentiv i materialiv, 1944-1961* (Ukrainian SSR. Ministry of Foreign Affairs. Ukrainian SSR on the international arena: A collection of documents and materials, 1944-1961). Kiev: Derzhavne vydavnytstvo politychnoi literatury URSR, 1963.

Ukrains'ka SSR u mizhnarodnikh vidnosynakh (Ukrainian SSR in international relations). Edited by L. K. Palamarchuk. Kiev: Vydavnytstvo Akademii Nauk Ukrains'koi RSR, 1959.

United Nations. Atomic Energy Commission. *Official Records.* Fourth Year, No. 4, March 22, 1949; No. 8, July 29, 1949. Lake Success, New York.

— General Assembly. *Ad Hoc Political Committee. Summary Records of Meetings* 27 September- 7 December, 1949. Lake Success, New York.

— General Assembly. *Ad Hoc Political Committee. Annex to the Summary Records of Meetings,* Vol.I, 1949. Lake Success, New York.

— General Assembly. *First Committee. Summary Records of Meetings September 21-December 8, 1948;* Annexes to the Summary Records of Meetings, 1948. Lake Success, New York; Palais de Chaillot, Paris.

— General Assembly. *Official Records.* Third Session, Part I, November 4, 1948; Fourth Session, November 2, 1949; November 23, 1949; December 7, 1949; Annexes to the Summary Records of Meetings, 1948; Fourth Session, Supplement No. 15, 1949. Lake Success, New York; Palais de Chaillot, Paris.

— Security Council. *Journal of the Security Council.* First Year, No. 2, January 24, 1946; No. 10, February 13, 1946; No. 11, February 15, 1946. Lake Success, New York.

— Security Council. *Official Records.* First Year, No. 4, August 28, 1946;

No. 7, September 3, 1946; No. 8, September 4, 1946; No. 9, September 5, 1946; No. 10, September 9, 1946; No. 11, September 13, 1946; No. 13, September 16, 1946; No. 14, September 16, 1946; No. 16, September 20, 1946. Third Year, Nos. 16-35, February 20, 1948; Nos. 36-51, March 17, 1948; No. 47, March 22, 1948; No. 51, March 31, 1948; No. 56, April 12, 1948; No. 63, April 29, 1948; No. 68, May 18, 1948; No. 69, May 19, 1948; No. 70, May 20, 1948; No. 72, May 22, 1948; No. 73, May 24, 1948; No. 75, May 27, 1948; No. 77, May 29, 1948; No. 86, June 17, 1948; No. 88, June 22, 1948; No. 91, July 1, 1948; No. 93, July 7, 1948; No. 95, July 13, 1948; No. 97, July 15, 1948; No. 101, August 4, 1948; No. 103, August 13, 1948; No. 104, August 16, 1948; No. 107, August 19, 1948; No. 118, October 19, 1948; No. 122, October 28, 1948; No. 123, October 29, 1948; No. 124, November 4, 1948; No. 135, December 27, 1948; No. 137, December 29, 1948. Fourth Year, No. 7, January 25, 1949; No. 9, January 29, 1949; No. 22, March 16, 1949; No. 42, September 15, 1949; No. 43, September 16, 1949; No. 51, December 12, 1949; No. 52, December 13, 1949. Supplements. First Year, No. 5, 1946. Third Year, January, February, March 1948; August 1948. Fourth Year, January, 1949; September, October, November, December 1949. Fifth Year, January, February, March 1950. Lake Success. New York; Palais de Chaillot, Paris.

United States. Department of State. Bureau of Intelligence and Research. *Status of the World's Nations* (Geographic Bulletin No. 2). Washington: U.S. Government Printing Office, 1967.

— Department of State. *Department of State Bulletin,* XI, No. 276, October 8, 1944; XII, No. 301, April 1, 1945; XII, No. 302, April 8, 1945; XII, no. 305, April 29, 1945. Washington: U.S. Government Printing Office.

— Department of State. *Foreign Relations of the United States: Diplomatic Papers, 1944,* Vol. I (General). Washington, Government Printing Office, 1966.

— Department of State. *Foreign Relations of the United States: Diplomatic Papers: The Conferences at Malta and Yalta.* Washington: U.S. Government Printing Office, 1955.

USSR. Akademiia Nauk. *Istoriia Sovetskoi Konstitutsii: Sbornik dokumentov, 1917-1957*(U.S.S.R. Academy of Sciences. History of the Soviet constitution: Collection of documents, 1917-1957). Moscow: Izdatel'stvo Akademii Nauk, 1957.

— Ministry of Foreign Affairs. *Correspondence between the Chairman of the Council of Ministers of the U.S.S.R. and the Presidents of the U.S.A. and the Prime Ministers of Grat Britain during the Great Patrioic War of 1941-1945.* London: Lawrence and Wishart, 1958.

Yearbook of the United Nations 1946-1947; 1947-1948; 1948-1949. Lake Success, New York.

Sbornik zakonov SSR i ukazov Presidiuma Verkhovnogo Soveta SSR (1938-July 1956) (Collection of laws and decrees of the Praesidium of the Supreme Soviet of the USSR (1938-July 1956). Moscow: Gosudarstvennoe izdatel'stvo iuridicheskoi literatury, 1956.

Books

Alker, Hayward R., and Russet, Bruce M. *World Politics in the General*

Assembly. New Haven: Yale University Press, 1965.

Ananov, I. N. *Ministerstva v SSSR* (Ministries in the USSR). Moscow: Gosudarstvennoe izdatel'stvo iuridicheskoi literatury, 1960.

Armstrong, Hamilton Fish. *Tito and Goliath.* New York: Macmillan, 1951.

Armstrong, John. *Ukrainian Nationalism.* 2d ed. New York: Columbia University Press, 1963.

Aspaturian, Vernon V. *The Union Republics in Soviet Diplomacy: A Study of Soviet Federalism in the Service of Soviet Foreign Policy.* Geneva: Librarie E. Droz, 1960.

Beitzell, Robert, ed. *Teheran, Yalta, Postdam: The Soviet Protocols.* Hattiesburg, Miss.: Academic International, 1970.

Bilinskyi, Yaroslav. *The Second Soviet Republic: The Ukraine after World War II.* New Brunswick: Rutgers University Press, 1964.

Bohlen, Charles E. *Witness to History, 1929-1969.* New York: W. W. Norton, 1973.

Boratynski, Stefan. *Dyplomacja okresu drugiej wojny swiatowej: Konferencje miedzynarodowe, 1941-1945* (Wyd. 1) (Diplomacy of the period of World War II: International conferences, 1941-1945). Warsaw: Panstwowe Wydawnictwo Naukowe, 1957.

Brierly, J. L. *The Law of Nations: An Introduction to the International Law of Peace.* 6th ed. Edited by Sir Humphrey Waldock. New York: Oxford University Press, 1963.

Brovka, Y. P. *Mezhdunarodnaia pravosub'ektnost' BSSR* (International legal subjectivity of BSSR). Minsk: Izdatel'stvo "Nauka i Tekhnika," 1967.

Byrnes, James F. *All in One Lifetime.* New York: Harper Brothers, 1958.

— *Speaking Frankly.* New York: Harper Brothers, 1947.

Chaning-Pearce, M., ed. *Federal Union: A Symposium.* London: Jonathan Cape, 1940.

Churchill, Winston S. *The Second World War.* Vol. VI: *Triumph and Tragedy.* Boston: Houghton Mifflin, 1953.

Claude, Inis L. *Swords into Ploughshares: The Problems and Progress of International Organization.* New York: Random House, 1956.

Clemens, Diane Shaver. *Yalta.* New York: Oxford University Press, 1970.

Conquest, Robert. *The Nation Killers: The Soviet Deportation of Nationalities.* New York: Macmillan, 1970.

Dallin, Alexander. *German Rule in Russia, 1941-1945: A Study of Occupation Policies.* London: Macmillan, 1957.

— *The Soviet Union at the United Nations: An Inquiry into Soviet Motives and Objectives.* New York: Praeger, 1962.

Dedijer, Vladimir. *The Battle Stalin Lost: Memoirs of Yugoslavia, 1948-1953.* New York: Grosset and Dunlap, 1971.

Djilas, Milovan. *Conversations with Stalin.* New York: Harcourt, Brace and World, 1962.

Duroselle, Jean-Baptiste. *Le conflit de Trieste, 1943-1954.* Brussels: Institut sociologique de li'Universite Libre de Bruxelles, 1966.

Dzyuba, Ivan. *Internationalism or Russification? A Study in the Soviet Nationalities Problem.* 2d ed. London: Weidenfeld and Nicolson, 1968.

Eban, Abba. *Voice of Israel.* New York: Horizon Press, 1957.

Eden, Anthony. *The Memoirs of Anthony Eden.* Vol. III: *The Reckoning.* Boston: Houghton Mifflin, 1965.

Fainsod, Merle. *How Russia Is Ruled.* Cambridge: Harvard University Press, 1956.

Fedorov, V. N. *Sovet Bezopasnosti OON* (Security Council of the United Nations). Moscow: Izdatel'stvo "Mezhdunarodnye otnosheniia," 1965.

Feis, Herbert. *Churchill, Roosevelt, Stalin: The War They Waged and the Peace They Sought.* Princeton: Princeton University Press, 1957.

Fenwick, Charles. *International Law.* 4th ed. New York: Appleton, Century, Crofts, 1965.

Fischer, Louis. *The Soviets in World Affairs: A History of the Relations between the Soviet Union and the Rest of the World, 1917-1929.* 2 vols. Princeton: Princeton University Press, 1951.

Fontaine, Andre. *History of the Cold War from the October Revolution to the Korean War, 1917-1950.* Translated from the French by D. D. Paige. New York: Pantheon Books, 1968.

Goodman, Elliot R. *The Soviet Design for a World State.* New York: Columbia University Press, 1960.

Goodrich, Leland. *The United Nations.* New York: Thomas Y. Crowell, 1959.

Gould, Wesley L. *An Introduction to International Law.* New York: Harper Brothers, 1957.

Hackworth, Green Haywood. *Digest of International Law.* Vol. I. Washington: U.S. Government Printing Office, 1949.

Halle, Louis J. *The Cold War as History.* New York: Harper and Row, 1967.

Hazard, John N. *The Soviet System of Government.* Rev. ed. Chicago: University of Chicago Press, 1960.

Hull, Cordell. *The Memoirs of Cordell Hull.* 2 vols. New York: Macmillan, 1948.

Hyamson, A. M. *Palestine under the Mandate, 1920-1948.* London: Methuen, 1951.

Indrtikh, Vesioly. *Khronika fevral'skikh dnei 1948 g. v Chekhoslovakii.* (Chronicle of February days of 1948 in Czechoslovakia). Moscow: Gosudarstvennoe izdatel'stvo politicheskoi literatury, 1960.

Moscow: Gosudarstvennoe izdatel'stvo politicheskoi literatury, 1960.

Inkeles, Alex, and Geiger, Kent. *Soviet Society: A Book of Readings.* Boston: Houghton Mifflin, 1961.

Israelian, V.L. *Diplomaticheskaia istoriia Velikoi Otechestvennoi Voiny, 1941-1945.* (Diplomatic history of the Great Patriotic War, 1941-1945). Moscow: Institut mezhdunarodnykh otnoshenii, 1959.

Istoriia Chekhoslovakii, (History of Czechoslovakia). Vol. III. Moscow: Izdatel'stvo Akademii Nauk SSSR, 1960.

Ivashin, I.F. *Ocherki istorii vneshnei politiki SSSR* (Outlines of the history of foreign policy of the USSR). Moscow: Gosudarstvennoe izdatel'stvo politicheskoi literatury, 1958.

Jessup, Philip C. *Modern Law of Nations: An Introduction.* New York: Macmillan, 1948.

Kahin, George McThurman. *Nationalism and Revolution in Indonesia.* Ithaca: Cornell University Press, 1952.

Kogan, Norman. *A Political History of Postwar Italy.* New York: Praeger, 1966.

Kolarz, Walter. *Russia and Her Colonies.* New York: Praeger, 1952.

Korbel, Josef. *The Communist Subversion of Czechoslovakia, 1938-1948.* Princeton: Princeton University Press, 1959.

Korowicz, Marek St. *Introduction to International Law: Present Conceptions of International Law in Theory and Practice.* The Hague: Martinus Nijhoff, 1959.

Kousoulas, George D. *Revolution and Defeat: The Story of the Greek Communist Party.* London: Oxford University Press, 1965.

Kozhevnikov, F. I., ed. *Mezhdunarodnoe pravo* (International law). Moscow: Gosudarstvennoe izdatel'stvo iuridicheskoi literatury, 1957.

Krasil'shchikova, S.A. *OON i natsional'no-osvoboditel'noe dvizhenie* (UN and national liberation movements). Moscow: Izdatel'stvo "Mezhdunarodnye otnosheniia," 1964.

Krylov. S. B. *Istoriia sozdaniia Organizatsii Ob'edinennykh Natsii* (History of the formation of the Organization of the United Nations). Moscow: Izdatel'stvo "Mezhdunarodnye otnosheniia," 1960.

Leahy, William D. *I Was There.* New York: Whittlesey House, 1950.

Levin, D. B. *Osnovnye problemy sovremennogo mezhdunarodnogo prava* (Basic problems of contemporary international law). Edited by D. A. Haidukova. Moscow: Gosudarstvennoe izdatel'stvo iuridicheskoi literatury, 1958.

Lieberman, Joseph I. *The Scorpion and the Tarantula: The Struggle to Control Atomic Weapons, 1945-1949.* Boston: Houghton Mifflin, 1970.

Lisovskii, B. U. *Mezhdunarodnoe pravo* (International law). Kiev: Izdatel'stvo kievs'kogo gosudarstvennogo universiteta im. T. Shevchenko, 1955.

Lynev, A. E. *Administrativnoe pravo* (Administrative law). Moscow: Izdatel'stvo "Iuridicheskaia literatura," 1967.

Macmahon, Arthur W., ed. *Federalism, Mature and Emergent.* Garden City: Doubleday, 1955.

McKenzie, Kermit E. *Comintern and World Revolution: The Shaping of a Doctrine.* London, New York: Columbia University Press, 1964.

Meigs, Cornelia. *The Great Design: Men and Events in the United Nations from 1945 to 1963.* Boston: Little Brown, 1964.

Mendlowitz, Saul H. *Legal and Political Problems of World Order.* New York: Fund for Education Concerning World Peace through Law, 1962.

Meyer, Alfred G. *The Soviet Political System: An Interpretation.* New York: Random House, 1965.

Mileikovskii, A. G., ed. *Mezdunarodnye otnosheniia posle Vtoroi Mirovoi Voiny,* (International relations after the Second World War). Vol. I Moscow: Gosudarstvennoe izdatel'stvo politicheskoi literatury, 1962.

Mirchuk, Petro. *Ukrains'ka Povstans'ka Armiia, 1942-1952.* (Ukrainian Insurgent Army, 1942-1952). Munich: Druckerei "Cicero," 1953.

Modzhorian, L. A., *Sub'ekty mezhdunarodnogo prava* (Subjects of international law). Moscow: Gosudarstvennoe izdatel'stvo iuridicheskoi literatury, 1958.

Morgenthau, Hans J. *Politics among Nations: The Struggle for Power and Peace.* 4th ed. New York: Knopf, 1967.

Morozov, G. U. *Organizatsiia Ob'edinennykh Natsii* (United Nations organization). Moscow: Izdatel'stvo "Mezhdunarodnye otnosheniia," 1960.

Morray, Joseph P. *From Yalta to Disarmament: Cold War Debate.* New York: M. R. Press, 1961.

Moseley, Philip E. *The Kremlin and World Politics: Studies in Soviet Policy.*

and Action. New York: Vintage, 1960.

Noel-Baker, Philip. *The Arms Race: A Programme for World Disarmament.* New York: Atlantic Books, 1958.

Nollau, Günther. *Die Internationale: Wurzeln und Erscheinungsformen des Proletarischen Internationalismus.* Köln: Verlag für Politik und Wirtschaft, 1959.

Notter, Harley A. *Postwar Foreign Policy Preparation.* Washington: U.S. Government Printing Office, 1949.

Novak, Bogdan C. *Trieste, 1941-1954: The Ethnic, Political and Ideological Struggle.* Chicago: University of Chicago Press, 1970.

O'Ballance, Edgar. *The Greek Civil War, 1944-1949.* New York: Praeger, 1966.

Palmier, Leslie H. *Indonesia and the Dutch.* London: Oxford University Press, 1962.

Pipes, Richard. *The Formation of the Soviet Union: Communism and Nationalism, 1917-1923.* Rev. ed. Cambridge: Harvard University Press, 1964.

Polk, William R. *United States and the Arab World.* Cambridge: Harvard University Press, 1965.

Reitlinger, Gerald. *House Built on Sand: The Conflicts of German Policy in Russia, 1939-1945.* London: Weidenfeld and Nicolson, 1960.

Ripka, Hubert. *Czechoslovakia Enslaved: The Story of the Communist Coup d'Etat.* London: Gollancz, 1950.

Roosevelt, Franklin Delano. *The Public Papers and Addresses of Franklin Delano Roosevelt.* Vol. XIII: *1944-1945. Victory and the Threshold of Peace.* Compiled by Samuel I. Rosenman. New York: Harper Brothers, 1950.

Schuschnigg, Kurt, von. *International Law: An introduction to the Law of Peace.* Milwaukee: Bruce Publishing Company, 1959.

Seabury, Paul. *Rise and Decline of the Cold War.* New York: Basic Books, 1967.

Sherwood, Robert Aura. *Philippine Freedom, 1946-1958.* New York: Columbia University Press, 1958.

Snell, John L., ed. *The Meaning of Yalta.* Baton Rouge: Louisiana State University Press, 1956.

Stettinius, Edward R. *Roosevelt and the Russians: The Yalta Conference.* Garden City: Doubleday, 1949.

Strausz-Hupe, Robert, and Possony, Stefan T. *International Relations in the Age of the Conflict between Democracy and Dictatorship.* New York: McGraw-Hill, 1954.

Sullivant, Robert S. *Soviet Politics and the Ukraine, 1917-1957.* New York: Columbia University Press, 1962.

Summers, Robert E., comp. *Dumbarton Oaks.* New York: H. W. Wilson, 1945.

Svarlien, Oscar. *An Introduction to the Law of Nations.* New York: McGraw-Hill, 1955.

Taracouzio, T. A. *The Soviet Union and International Law: A Study Based on the Legislation, Treaties and Foreign Relations of the Union of Soviet Socialist Republics.* New York: Macmillan, 1935.

Taranov, A. P. *Osnovni pryncypy konstytutsii Ukrains'koi RSR* (Basic principles of the constitution of the Ukrainian SSR). Kiev: Vydavnytstvo

Akademii Nauk Ukrainskoi RSR, 1962.

Taylor, Alastair May. *Indonesian Independence and the United Nations.* Ithaca: Cornell University Press, 1960.

Tomko, Y. *Vnutrenniaia kompetentsiia gosudarstv i Organizatsiia Ob'edinnennykh Natsii* (Domestic competence of states and the United Nations Organization). Translated from the Slovak by O. F. Sakun. Moscow: Izdatel'stvo inostrannoi literatury, 1963.

Towster, Julian. *Political Power in the U.S.S.R. 1917-1947: The Theory and Structure of Government in the Soviet State.* New York: Oxford University Press, 1948.

Truman, Harry S. *Memoirs of Harry S. Truman.* Vol. I. *Year of Decisions.* Garden City: Doubleday, 1955.

Tys-Krochmaliuk, Yuriy. *UPA Warfare in Ukraine: Strategical, Tactical and Organizational Problems of Ukrainian Resistance in World War II.* New York: Society of Veterans of Ukrainian Insurgent Army of the United States and Canada and St. George the Victorious Association of Veterans of Ukrainian Insurgent Army in Europe, 1972.

Ukrainian SSR. Akademiia Nauk. Institut Istorii. *Ukrains'kaia SSR i zarubezhnye sotsialisticheskie strany.* (Ukrainian SSR and foreign socialist countries). Kiev: Izdatel'stvo "Naukova Dumka," 1965.

Ulam, Adam B. *Expansion and Coexistence, The History of Soviet Foreign Policy 1917-1967.* New York: Praeger, 1968.

United Nations and Disarmament, 1945-1965, The. New York: United Nations Office of Public Information, 1967.

Vandenberg, Arthur H., Jr., ed., with the collaboration of Joe Alex Morris. *The Private Papers of Senator Vandenberg.* Boston: Houghton Mifflin, 1952.

Vlasov, V. A., and Studenikin, S. S. *Sovetskoe administrativenoe pravo* (Soviet administrative law). Moscow, Gosudarstvennoe izdatel'stvo iuridicheskoi literatury, 1959.

von Schuschnigg, Kurt. *International Law: An Introduction to the Law of Peace.* Milwaukee: Bruce Publishing Company, 1959.

Vyshinskii, Andrei Y., ed. *The Law of the Soviet State.* Translated from the Russian by Hugh W. Babb with introduction by John N. Hazard. New York: Macmillan, 1948.

Wheare, K. C. *Federal Government.* 3rd ed. with introduction by John N. Hazard. London: Oxford University Press, 1953.

Williams, L. F. R. *The State of Israel.* New York: Macmillan, 1957.

Wolf, Charles, Jr. *Indonesian Story: The Birth, Growth and Structure of the Indonesian Republic.* New York: John Day, 1948.

Woodward, Llewellyn E. *British Foreign Policy in the Second World War.* London: Her Majesty's Stationary Office, 1962.

Wright, Michael. *Disarm and Verify: An Explanation of the Central Difficulties of National Policies.* New York: Praeger, 1964.

Xydis, Stephen G. *Greece and the Great Powers, 1944-1947: Prelude to the Truman Doctrine.* Thessaloniki: Institute for Balkan Studies, 1963.

Yurchenko, O. *Pryroda i funktsiia sovets'kykh federatyvnykh form* (The nature and function of the Soviet federative forms). Munich: Institute for the Study of the USSR, 1956.

Zavialov, B. *Dmytro Zakharovych Manuilsky.* Kiev: Vydavnytstvo politychnoi literatury, 1967.

Zlatopol'skii, D. L. *Gosudarstvennoe ustroistvo SSR.* (State structure of the U.S.S.R.). Moscow: Gosudarstvennoe izdatel'stvo iuridicheskoi literatury, 1960.

Articles and Periodicals

De Visscher, Paul. ''A propos de la personnalite juridique de l'Ukraine.'' *L'Ukraine dans le cadre de l'Est Europeen.* Louvain: Editions Nauwelaerts, 1957.

Dolan, Edward. ''The Member-Republics of the U.S.S.R. as Subjects of the Law of Nations.'' *The International and Comparative Law Quarterly,* IV (1955).

Halaichuk, Bohdan T. ''Has the United States Recognized Ukraine?'' *Ukrainian Quarterly,* XI, No. 1, (1955).

— ''The Soviet Ukraine as a Subject of International Law.'' *The Annals of the Ukrainian Academy of Arts and Sciences in the United States,* IX (1961).

Koretskyi, V. M. ''Mizhnarodno-pravna subektnist' Ukrains'koi RSR'' (International legal personality of the Ukrainian SSR). *Ukrains'ka Radians'ka Sotsialistychna Respublika.* (Ukrainian Soviet Socialist Republic). Kiev: Akademiia Nauk Ukrains'koi RSR, 1965.

Kurishkov, E. L. ''Pro mizhnarodne predstavnytstvo Ukrains' koi RSR'' (About international representation of the Ukrainian SSR). *Visnyk Akademii Nauk Ukrains'koi RSR, No. 5 (1954).*

Ianovskii, M. N. ''Sovetskie soiuznye Respubliki—polnopravnye sub'ekty mezhdunarodnogo prava'' (Soviet Socialist Republics — Full subjects of international law). *Sovetskoe gosudarstvo i pravo,* XII (1962).

Lysyi, V.''Derzhavnyi status USSR ta inshykh soiuznykh Respublik SSSR.'' *Vilna Ukraina,* No. 34 (1962).

New York Times, The. February 11, 1946; September 5, 1946; March 13, 14, 1948; July 8, 9, 1949.

Radians'ka Ukraina. April 28, 29, 1945; May 8, 9, 1945; September 13, 1946.

Udovychenko, P. ''Ukrains'ka RSR v OON'' (Ukrainian SSR in the UN). *Radians'ke pravo,* No. 3 (1966).

Ul'ianova, N.M. ''Mizhnarodni dohovory Radians'koi Ukrainy'' (International treaties of Soviet Ukraine). *Radians'ke pravo,* No. 11 (1966).

— ''Uchast' Ukrains'koi RSR u mizhnarodnikh konferentsiiakh i mizhnarodikh dohovorakh'' (Participation of the Ukrainian SSR in international conferences and treaties). M. P. Bazhan *et al. Ukrains'ka Radians'ka Sotsialistychna Respublika.* Kiev: Akademiia Nauk Ukrains'koi RSR, 1965.

Verdross, Alfred, ''Die Völkerrechtssubjektivitat der Gliedstaaten der Sowjetunion'' *Osterreichische Zeitschrift fur Offentliches Rect,* I, (1946).

Pamphlets

Boborov, R. L., and Malinin S. A. *Organizatsiia Ob'edinnennykh Natsii* (United Nations organization). Leningrad: Izdatel'stvo Leningradskogo Universiteta, 1960.

Holub, Vsevolod. *Ukraina v Ob'ednanykh Natsiakh.* (Ukraine in the United Nations). Munich: ''Suchasna Ukraina,'' 1953.

Soviet Union at the San Francisco Conference. London: ''Soviet News,'' 1945.

Yakemtchouk, Romain. *L'Ukraine en droit international.* Louvain: Centre ukrainien d'etudes en Belgique, 1954.

Other Sources

Bol'shaia Sovetskaia Entsiklopediia. 2d ed. Moscow: Izdatel'stvo "Sovetskaia Entsiklopedia," 1954.

Diplomaticheskii Slovar'. Moscow: Gosudarstvennoe izdatel'stvo politicheskoi literatury, 1960-1964. 3 vols.

Sovetskaia Istoricheskaia Entsiklopedia. (Moscow: Izdatel'stvo i "Sovetskaia Entsiklopedia," 1961.

Ukrains'ka Radians'ka Entsyklopedia. Vol. VIII. Kiev: Akademiia Nauk Ukrains'koi Radians'koi Sotsialistychnoi Respubliky, 1962.

INDEX

EAST EUROPEAN MONOGRAPHS

1. Political Ideas and the Enlightenment in the Romanian Principalities, 1750-1831. By Vlad Georgescu. 1971.

2. America, Italy and the Birth of Yugoslavia, 1917-1919. By Dragan R. Zivojinovic. 1972.

3. Jewish Nobles and Geniuses in Modern Hungary. By William O. McCagg, Jr. 1972.

4. Mixail Soloxov in Yugoslavia: Reception and Literary Impact. By Robert F. Price. 1973.

5. The Historical and Nationalistic Thought of Nicolae Iorga. By William O. Oldson. 1973.

6. Guide to Polish Libraries and Archives. By Richard C. Lewanski. 1974.

7. Vienna Broadcasts to Slovakia, 1938-1939: A Case Study in Subversion. By Henry Delfiner. 1974.

8. The 1917 Revolution in Latvia. By Andrew Ezergailis. 1974.

9. The Ukraine in the United Nations Organization: A Study in Soviet Foreign Policy, 1944-1950. By Konstantyn Sawczuk. 1975.